Number Idioms: Hole in One!

English Number Idioms Explained, with Multiple Examples, Exercises, and Puzzles

John Sailors

Targets in English

Targets in English

ISBN-13: 978-1-938688-09-6

Page design by Targets in English.
This book is set in Optima, an elegant, easy-to-read
sans serif typeface with thick-thin contrast.

Find Us:
TargetsinEnglish.com
Twitter.com/TargetsEnglish
Facebook.com/TargetsInEnglish

May we all find our Cloud Nine!

Contents

Introduction: Learning Idioms by Topic

Idioms are phrases whose meanings are not clear from the words they contain. For instance, the phrase *hole in one* means "a great success." It comes from golf, a sport in which the greatest achievement is hitting a ball into a hole in only one stroke. The phrase is also used figuratively, for achievements outside of golf.

Idioms come from many soures: talk about sports, money, foods, etc.; from proverbs and old sayings; from the Bible and religion; and from famous writers such as Shakespeare, who invented numerous English idioms.

Idioms make the English language colorful, giving speakers and writers new ways to express ideas.

For learners of English, however, idioms are *a pain in the neck* (an idiom meaning "a lot of trouble"). This is because there are thousands and thousands of them to learn.

One solution is to learn idioms by topic, such as sports idioms, money idioms, and, here, number idioms, or phrases that have numbers in them. What does it mean, for example, if you are *one in a million*? What is the difference between *one of these days* and *one of those days*? And when people can hear and understand something, why do they say *Ten-four*?

By learning these idioms together, students will be able to more-easily understand the phrases and remember them later, with one phrase bringing others to mind.

This book teaches idioms by topic—numbers—and also serves as a reference book, a dictionary students can use later. An alphabetical list of idioms covered is located in the back.

Readers are guaranteed to find themselves *in seventh heaven* or *on cloud nine* when they're done.

How to Use This Book

Number Idioms: Hole in One! teaches more than 200 common phrases selected after careful research in idiom and phrasal verb dictionaries, standard dictionaries, and online sources. The book offers a dictionary format with several valuable features, including detailed definitions, explanations of phrase origins, and two example sentences for each idiom. It also provides exercises, puzzles, and examples from real news headlines.

Definitions. Dictionaries sometimes disagree on definitions of idioms and how they are used. To ensure accuracy, this book's definitions were written after thorough research in numerous sources, among them:
• The Oxford English Dictionary.
• Merriam-Webster.com.
• The American Heritage Dictionary.
• The American Heritage Dictionary of Idioms (Ammer).
• Webster's New World Dictionary.
• Collins Cobuild Dictionary.
• MacmillanDictionary.com.
• Cambridge Learner's Dictionary.
• Various idiom and phrasal verb dictionaries.

Spelling. Merriam-Webster's served as the spelling authority for this book, as it is for much of the American publishing world (not including news organizations, which use Webster's New World for spelling).

Explanations. Where possible, the origins and sometimes dates of phrases are offered. This information came from the massive Oxford English Dictionary and other sources.

Examples. Two example sentences are given for each idiom to best illustrate how phrases are commonly used, as determined with research into examples offered in dictionaries and authentic instances found in word banks. In addition, instances of idioms appearing in news headlines are scattered throughout the book.

Sections. The book is divided into seven sections, with a list of idioms at the beginning and a page of exercises at the end. An Answer Key for all of exercises and puzzles can be found in the back.

Parts-of-speech labels. Most idiom dictionaries do not offer parts-of-speech labels, since these are not exact and are often difficult to assign. This book offers them, however, since the labels are very useful for learners. Keep in mind, they serve only as a guide to help readers see how phrases are used. Here is a key:

- *v. phr.* = verb phrase
- *adj. phr.* = adjective phrase
- *phrasal verb* = (just that)
- *clause* = (just that)
- *n. phr.* = noun phrase
- *adv. phr.* = adverb phrase
- *phr.* = *phrase*

V. phr. vs. phrasal verb. A *verb phrase* is a group of words that functions as a verb. *Phrasal verbs* are verbs with *particles* (prepositions and prepositional adverbs such as *in, out, up, etc.*).

The abbreviation *phr.* (phrase) in this book is used for idioms that do not fit any identifiable parts-of-speech function in sentences. *Clause* is used for idioms that form a complete sentence.

One vs. someone. (*One*) is used in idioms such as *(one's) better half* to refer to the subject of the sentence, while *(someone)* refers to a person other than the subject, as in *have (someone's) number.*

Studying. Start by going over the idioms at the beginning of each section. Underline idioms you don't know and then try to guess their meaning by looking at their words. Next, read through and study the section, and then do the exercises at the end. Finally, return to the idioms list to review.

Reference. This book is designed with two purposes: (1) A textbook for class or individual use and (2) a reference book for students. An alphabetical list of the book's idioms is located in the back.

Section 1

We begin with idioms containing the words *number, zero,* and *half.* By learning these phrases together, students will be able to better understand and more-easily remember them.

Go over the idioms below and underline any that you don't recognize. Then try to guess their meaning by looking at the words that make them up. What do you think it means to *crunch numbers*? Is it good or bad to *look out for number one*? Thinking about the idioms and the words they contain is *half the battle*

- by the numbers
- number cruncher
- (one's) days are numbered
- do a number on
- in round numbers
- look out for number one
- safety in numbers
- zero in on
- with half a heart
- go halfway
- the half of it
- not half bad
- have half a mind
- see with half an eye
- any number of
- crunch numbers
- (one's) number is up
- get/have (someone's) number
- number one
- opposite number
- zero hour
- go from zero to hero
- half a loaf is better than none
- go halves
- half the battle
- give/have half a chance
- glass is half full
- (one's) better half

Study the following pages until you get to the Review and Practice section on page 22. After completing that, return to the list above and review idioms you underlined.

— Number —

The English word *number* comes from French, and before that the Latin *numerus*, meaning "quantity." The word is similar in numerous European languages: *número* (Spanish/Portuguese), *nombre* (French), *numero* (Italian), *nummer* (German, Danish) …

An old word, it also appears in *any number of* idioms.

COUNTING

1.
by the numbers *adv. phr.*

Step by step, in the correct order. This idiom comes from the military. It uses *number* to mean "the order things should be done in." Similar: *by the book.* Opposite: *by the seat of (one's) pants.*

- Read the instructions when you put the computer together. Do it by the numbers.
- Our old manager insisted we do everything by the book, not by the seat of our pants.

2.
any number of *phr.*

Several, many; an unknown number. Likely more than one.

- Helen might have heard the news from any number of people.
- You could run into any number of problems when you move to New York. Big cities are hard to get used to.

> **Compare:** *A number of* means simply "many" or "numerous." Adding *any* (*any number of*), means that the number is unknown. Consider these examples:
>
> - Mike may have quit his job for *a number of* reasons. (He may have quit for two or more reasons.)
> - Mike may have quit for any number of reasons. (We don't know why Mike quit his job.)

3.
number cruncher *n. phr.*

A person whose job is to work with large amounts of numbers. This idiom comes from computers. The phrase was used by the 1960s to mean a computer or software that could make fast calculations. By 1971 the idiom was used in accounting and statistics. See also: *crunch numbers* (below).

- I was so sorry to see our company accountant quit. She was the best number cruncher we ever had.
- I hate working on my income taxes; I'm a terrible number cruncher.

4.
crunch numbers *v. phr.*

To work with or examine large amounts of numbers. By the 1970s people began to use the verb *number-crunch* and then just *crunch,* as in *crunch numbers.* Today it's used for any kind of work with numbers, even one's own finances. See also: *number cruncher* (above).

- Our accountant spent several long days crunching numbers to decide how much money our company could invest in the project.
- Mary wanted to crunch some numbers before she decided which house to buy.

FINISHED

5.
(one's) days are numbered *clause.*

(1) One will not be in a job or position for long. (2) One will not live much longer. Here, *number* is used as a verb (passive voice). Similar: *(one's) number is up* (below). Colloquial/slang.

- I think our manager's days (at this company) are numbered. He's just not doing very well.
- I knew my car's days were numbered, so I began saving money to buy a new one.

6.

(one's) number is up   *clause.*

(1) One is near death. (2) One is close to losing a job or position. This idiom originally referred to a lottery number, but the phrase soon was used figuratively. Similar: *(one's) days are numbered* (above). Colloquial/slang.

- By the time we arrived at the hospital, it was clear the patient's number was up.
- Jake knew his number was up at the company when he saw his manager's face.

7.

do a number on   *v. phr.*

(1) To harm. (2) To trick or cheat. This informal idiom is used mainly in American English. Colloquial/slang.

- Jill's friends did a number on the house. It was a mess.
- Be careful. This windy weather will do a number on your hair. You may want to wear a hat.

8.

get/have (someone's) number   *v. phr.*

To learn (get) or know (have) someone's true motive or goal. *Number* here is used in the sense of "appraisal" (estimate of how much money something is worth). The phrase goes back to at least the 1850s. Colloquial/slang.

- The salesman couldn't fool me. I had his number.
- I got his number a long time ago. I know I can't trust him.

9.

in round numbers   *phr.*

An estimate, an approximate number. This idiom uses *round* in the sense of "round off," or "inexact number" (for example, 1,800 instead of 1,807). Also: *in round figures.* Similar: *ballpark figure.*

- In round numbers, I'd say the car is worth a couple thousand.
- She didn't need an exact figure. She said an estimate in round numbers would be OK (... a ballpark figure would be OK).

NUMBERS AS PEOPLE

10.
number one *n. phr.*

The best, the most liked, or the highest ranked. This idiom is often abbreviated: "No. 1." Also an adjective.

- Mary is number one in tennis.
- Our team came in at number one this year. We're the number one team.

> **No. 1:** *Number one* is an idiom in many languages. The Spanish *numero uno*, meaning "best," is used in English and listed in English dictionaries. The Japanese *ichiban* means "the best" or "wonderful." It's uncommon in English but is listed in English dictionaries. Note, other numbers can be spelled with *No.*: No. 1, No. 2, No. 723, etc.

11.
look out for number one *v. phr.*

To think mainly of oneself and not others. This idiom is often negative to say people care only about themselves. *Number one* goes back to at least 1705: "The Knight I doubt not, but 'tis very careful of number one, and looks no further." Colloquial.

- Betty is a terrible mayor; she only looks out for number one.
- A good manager doesn't just look out for number one.

12.
opposite number *n. phr.*

A person in another department, company, or organization who has one's same rank or position. This idiom was recorded in 1874 for a position on fishing boats.

- Store managers meet one weekend every year to share ideas with their opposite numbers.
- The mayor met with his opposite number while visiting New York City. (He met New York's mayor.)

13.
safety in numbers *phr.*

It's safer to be in a group or with more than one person. This idiom comes from a Latin proverb that refers to military situations, when more people is of course better.

- The woods can be dangerous at night, so stay together. There's safety in numbers.
- The old saying "There's safety in numbers" may be very useful today.

Idioms in the News

🖎 "Most people encounter soy through **any number of** food products." (They get soy beans in an unknown number of products such as soy sauce, edamame, etc.)
—Washington Post, July 26, 2018.

🖎 "A significant share of people who **crunch numbers** for a living use Microsoft Excel or other spreadsheet programs like Google Sheets."
—Quartz, Sept. 22, 2017.

🖎 "**Days are numbered** for ATMs in Japan's banking system." (Soon Japan will have no automatic teller machines.)
—Japan Times, June 8, 2018.

🖎 "People think **in round numbers** when asked how much they want to save ..." (They don't have exact numbers in mind.)
—Forbes, Feb. 4, 2019.

🖎 "Nintendo Will Take the **Number One** Spot from Sony In 2019." (The Nintendo video game console will be the most popular by sales.)
—Business Wire (press release), Nov. 29, 2018.

— Zero —

The word *zero* is a noun, a verb, and an adjective.

- Noun: A computer uses ones and zeros.
  (zeros or zeroes)
- Verb: Our company is zeroing in on smartphone apps.
  (zero, zeros, zeroing, zeroed) (No. 15 below.)
- Adjective: Paul has zero tolerance for noise.

14.

zero hour *n. phr.*

(1) A time when an important decision must be made. (2) A time when a military action is scheduled; a time when an important event is scheduled. Originally a military term that was soon used figuratively.

- Are all the musicians ready? It's almost zero hour—the concert is about to begin.
- Sorry, it's zero hour. We must make our decision now.

15.

zero in (on) *phrasal verb.*

(1) To aim at with a gun. (2) To turn one's attention to something. This idiom was originally used for guns, but soon was used for aiming one's attention.

- The new mayor promised to zero in on crime.
- When John turned on the cartoon, the kids zeroed in on the TV.

16.

go from zero to hero *v. phr.*

To suddenly become very popular, often after being very unpopular. Adjective: *zero-to-hero*.

- The new president went from zero to hero when she cut taxes.
- We hated our professor until he canceled the exam. Then he went from zero to hero. It was a zero-to-hero decision.

— Half —

Half is a noun and an adjective. The verb is *halve*.

- Noun: half the distance, half past two (2:30). (plural: halves)
- Adjective: a half sheet of paper, a half mile.
- Verb: The store halved its prices. (halve, halves, halved, halving)

Note that adjective phrases with *half* are often hyphenated: *half-asleep, half-finished;* but not noun phrases: *a half sister, a half hour, half a sandwich.* Some phrases are closed: *halfway, halfhearted (or half-hearted).*

17.

(with) half a heart   *adv. phr.*

With only a little enthusiasm. Unenthusiastically. Also: *half-hearted* is an adjective, and *half-heartedly* is an adverb. The opposite is *with all (one's) heart.*

- After she sold her company, Karen continued to manage it, but she worked with only half a heart.
- Kim is hoping with all her heart that she'll get the job she applied for yesterday.

COOPERATING

18.

half a loaf is better than none   *clause.*

It is better to have something, even if that something is less than one wanted. This expression refers to a loaf of bread. As a proverb it goes back to at least 1546: "For better is halfe a lofe than no bread" (old spellings).

- I know you really wanted a sports car, one that's fast, but this car's not bad, and it's inexpensive. Half a loaf is better than none.
- We must all learn to compromise. We can't have everything. And remember, half a loaf is better than none.

19.

go halfway *v. phr.*

To compromise. To give up something to solve a disagreement. A similar idiom is *meet someone halfway*. These idioms picture the middle between two different opinions. A related term is *middle ground,* which means a compromise that both sides can accept.

- Hal and Sharon both wanted to hold our company party at their houses, so they went halfway: The party was at Sharon's house, but Hal cooked the food.
- A good politician must learn to meet others halfway. It's better to find a middle ground. Often, half a loaf is better than none.

20.

go halves *v. phr.*

To share equally, to split the costs of something. This idiom goes back to at least the late 1600s. An idiom with the same meaning is *go fifty-fifty*. For restaurants and dates, the phrase *go Dutch* is also commonly used.

- Mike and Jim decided that if they went halves, they could afford an inexpensive car and start driving to work.
- My roommate and I agreed to go halves (go fifty-fifty) on the apartment's rent and also on all bills.

21.

the half of it *n. phr.*

Only part of something, not the whole story. Often used in the negative: *not the half of it*.

- I knew our company's sales were down, but that was only the half of it. I learned that our manager is leaving soon, which will be even worse.
- "I hear Tom's moving to London!" "That's not the half of it. He's also getting married."

Idioms in the News

✎ "If you think getting into college is hard, you don't know **the half of it**." (It's even harder than you think.)

—Washington Post, Nov. 12, 2018.

22.

half the battle *n. phr.*

A successful start; success in a difficult part of a task. The word *battle* originally meant a fight in war, but is often used figuratively.

- Getting students to study regularly is half the battle. Once they have good habits, they are much easier to teach.
- We decided which neighborhood we want to live in, and when it comes to house hunting, that's half the battle.

23.

not half bad *adj. phr.*

Quite good. This and similar idioms call something good by saying it isn't bad: *not bad, not too bad, not too shabby.* (*Shabby* means "old and worn out," as in clothes or a building.) Colloquial.

- We were worried when John said he was going to learn to cook, but he makes dinner every night now, and his cooking isn't half bad.
- "How's the coffee?" "Not bad. Really, not half bad."

24.

give/have half a chance *v. phr.*

If someone has or is given an opportunity, the person will certainly take it. Also just *give/have a chance.*

- Please keep the door closed. If you give my cat half a chance, she'll run outside.
- Sheila knew the company would hire her, if they would just give her a chance to show her computer skills.

25.

have half a mind *v. phr.*

To want to do something, to be inclined. Similar expressions include *have a good/great mind (to)* and just *have a mind to.*

- The service in this restaurant is slow! I have half a mind to complain to the manager.
- Musicians were making so much money in Kansas City, Pete had a good mind to move there himself.

26.
glass is half full *clause.*

An optimistic outlook. Optimistic (half full) and pessimistic (half empty). This phrase comes from the common expression "Is the glass half empty or half full?" meaning, Are you a pessimist or an optimist?

- When she learned their plane would be two hours late, Shelly smiled and said, "Well, more time for duty-free shopping (shopping with no taxes) in the airport." To Shelly, the glass is always half full; there's always a silver lining (a good side).
- My manager says she only hires employees who see the glass as half-full.

> **Optimists:** The adjectives are *optimistic* and *pessimistic*. The nouns (outlook) are *optimism* and *pessimism*. The people are *optimists* and *pessimists*.
>
> - Ron dislikes pessimism. He thinks pessimists are irritating. He doesn't like pessimistic people.

27.
see with half an eye *v. phr.*

To notice easily, with just a glance or quick look. This idiom refers to an eye being half-open. It goes back to at least the 1530s. From 1651: "Any one may see with half an eye, how impertinent it is."

- The waiter could see with half an eye that the customers were unhappy, even though they tried to be polite.
- We could see with half an eye that it was not a good hotel.

28.
(one's) better half *n. phr.*

One's spouse (husband or wife). This old idiom is used lightly in conversation for "husband" or "wife." Colloquial.

- Hey, Sarah, how come you didn't bring your better half?
- Let me introduce you to my better half.

Idioms in the News

✎ "Your **better half** can make golf more enjoyable." (Advice to male golfers: Invite your wife to golf with you.)
—Daily Herald (Chicago), June 16, 2020.

✎ "Feds, province **go halves** on $394 million for affordable housing in Nova Scotia." (Canada's federal government and the Nova Scotia provincial government both are paying for this low-income housing.)
—Chronicle Herald (Nova Scotia), Aug. 20, 2019.

✎ "Scientists **Zero In on** Reefs With Best Chance of Survival." (As the world's ocean reefs die out because of global warming and other problems, scientists are studying reefs that can better survive (not die), hoping to learn how to save the reefs.)
—Oceans Deeply, Aug. 24, 2017.

✎ "How mosquitoes **zero in on** warm bodies." (Science feature explaining why it is that mosquitoes are attracted to people.)
—BBC News, July 16, 2015.

✎ "Nancy Pelosi reveals advice she received from UK **opposite number** John Bercow." (American politician gets advice from UK politician who holds the same position.)
—BBC News, April 16, 2019.

✎ "**From zero to hero**: The unlikely rise of Utah State linebacker Eric Munoz." (American football player at Utah State University has sudden, unexpected success.)
—Desert News (Utah, US), Nov. 17, 2019.

✎ "**Safety in Numbers**—Why Thousands of Birds Move as One." (Public radio podcast explaining why birds and fish travel together.)
—WBUR (Boston NPR), Mar. 1, 2017.

Crossword Puzzle

ACROSS

2. Eating less is only ___ the battle in losing weight. Exercise is needed too.

3. You can tell Mr. Smith doesn't like teaching history. He lectures with only half a ___.

6. Francine only cares about herself. She'll only ___ out for number one.

7. Ron's optimistic. To him the glass is always ___ full.

8. Hey, this soup is ___ half bad. You're a good cook.

9. My accountant will ___ some numbers to see how much we can spend.

13. Follow the instructions; do everything ___ numbers.

14. This week we focused on history; next week we'll ___ in on math.

15. Karen won! She is number ___.

16. It's time to start the meeting. It's zero ___.

17. Our mayor hoped to meet with her ___ number in New York, but the New York mayor was too busy.

DOWN

1. I've never met Tim's ___ half. What's his wife like?

2. If you two disagree, you should go ___ and find a middle ground.

4. Pessimists see a half glass of water as half ___.

5. This hotel isn't perfect, but it's OK. Half a ___ is better than none.

10. Our manager has made a lot of mistakes lately. I think her days here are ___.

11. When our leaders disagree, they should meet each other ___.

12. The unpopular president went from zero to ___ when he lowered taxes.

14. Peter has ___ tolerance for noise. He hates it.

Review and Practice

Test Your Memory

Choose the best answer.

1. Jill said, "He can't fool me! I've got his number." She means she ___.

   A. has his phone number
   B. knows his salary
   C. knows what he's trying to do

2. My father told me to look out for No. 1. This means I should ___.

   A. be loyal to my boss
   B. protect myself
   C. plan ahead and be ready

3. The mayor will meet with her opposite number in New York. She's going to meet with ___.

   A. her opponent
   B. someone very different
   C. New York's mayor

4. We have to decide now. It's ___.

   A. number one
   B. zero in
   C. zero hour

5. Dan worked here for a year before I met his better half, before I ___.

   A. saw his good side
   B. saw how experienced he was
   C. was introduced to his wife

6. The kids did a number on the kitchen. They ___.

   A. made it very clean
   B. messed it up
   C. cooked a big meal

7. "Who ate my cake?" "Any number of people could have eaten it." This means ___.

   A. two or less people
   B. a lot of different people
   C. only a few people

8. Let's split the dinner bill; let's ___.

   A. go halfway
   B. go halves
   C. do the half of it

Good or Bad

For each idiom, choose G for a good situation or B for a bad one. When finished see the Answer Key.

1. (one's) days are numbered ___

2. do a number on ___

3. safety in numbers ___

4. with half a heart ___

5. go halfway ___

6. not half bad ___

7. from zero to hero ___

8. glass is half empty ___

Quick Thought

As quickly as you can, think of an idiom that can have the following meanings. When finished, check the Answer Key.

1. split a restaurant bill

2. (do) reluctantly

3. suddenly become famous

4. tasty

5. focus on

6. harm

7. follow the rules

8. time to do something

Section 2

There is a 1972 film called *One Is a Lonely Number* and an old song called "One is the Loneliest Number." With idioms, though, *one* is far from lonely. There are many idioms that use *one*.

What, for example, is *A-one*? Or if we have to go *back to square one*, are we playing a game? And what's the difference between *one of these days* and *one of those days?*

Which of the following idioms is new to you? Underline each one that is new.

- A-one
- one too many
- at one fell swoop
- one up
- all one
- rolled up in one
- the one and only
- (all) in one piece
- one for the books
- it takes one to know one
- pull a fast one
- one of those days
- put all (one's) eggs in one basket
- one-man show

- at one (with)
- one-track mind
- back to square one
- go one better
- one and the same
- one of a kind
- one for the road
- hole in one
- in one ear and out the other
- wear more than one hat
- one of those things
- one of these days
- more than one way to skin a cat

Study the following pages until you get to Review and Practice on page 32. Then return to the list above to review the idioms you underlined.

— One —

The word *one* has numerous meanings. For instance it means "a single thing" or "exactly one." It also can mean "the only," as in "This is the one bus that will take us there," and mean "the right person to marry," as in "She knew he was the one."

One is also used in a great number of idioms and proverbs.

29.

A-one *adj. phr.*

Having the best-possible rating; first-class, high quality. This idiom comes from Lloyd's, the British insurance company. Beginning in 1775, the company classified ships that were in the best condition as "A1." Today *A-one* is used for all kinds of things. Spelled *A-1*, *A1*, or *A-one*.

- The restaurant down the street serves an A-one steak.
- The rooms at the resort were small but the service was A-1.

30.

at one (with) *phr.*

In agreement with, in harmony with. This idiom appeared in the thirteenth century and was for a time spelled as one word, *aton* or *at-on*.

- The two managers are not always at one on the best way to run their company.
- In the mountains, we felt truly at one with nature.

31.

one too many *n. phr.*

(1) One more than is wanted, needed, or beneficial. This idiom appeared in William Shakespeare's *Romeo and Juliet*. (2) One more alcoholic drink than is responsible. The latter is colloquial.

- Mike showed up to work late one too many times and got fired.
- I've had one too many (glasses of wine). I'd better call a taxi.

32.

one-track mind *n. phr.*

A mind that always thinks about one thing. This idiom comes from railroads. It refers to a train that runs only on one track or in one direction. This idiom was in use by 1915 to describe US President Woodrow Wilson: "I am afraid that the President's characterization of himself as 'a man with a one-track mind' is all too true."

- Many of our store's customers have a one-track mind: They just want to save money. They're not interested in fashion.
- My cat has a one-track mind. The only thing she ever wants to do is eat.

33.

at one fell swoop *adv. phr.*

All at once, with a single action. Sometimes used with *in: in one fell swoop.* With *fell* this idiom was probably created by Shakespeare in his play *Macbeth. Swoop* (verb, noun) means to suddenly move downward when flying, as a bird does. *Fell* at the time (1616) meant "deadly" or "cruel." However, today in this idiom *fell* has the meaning of "sudden." Similar idioms: *in one stroke, in one blow,* and *in a single blow.*

- When our CEO hired Shelly as our sales manager, he solved all our problems in one fell swoop.
- By accidentally erasing the computer file, he ruined hours of work at one fell swoop.

34.

back to square one *phr.*

One must start over because on the first try, one did not succeed. This idiom probably refers to board games that use squares to show players' progress. Similar: *back to the drawing board.*

- Oh no! We made a mistake when we put in the computer's motherboard, so it's back to square one. We have to take everything out and start over.
- Timmy gave the radio to his son to fix. When his son failed to repair it, he said, "I guess it's back to the drawing board."

35.

one up *adj. phr.*

To have an advantage over someone, to be ahead. This idiom comes from sports, where it means "one point ahead."

- Kim and I are both applying to become store manager, but Kim is one up on me—she has management experience.
- Our boss insists we always be one up on our competitors.

> **One-upmanship:** This is the practice of always trying to be *one up*, or at an advantage, over others. The behavior is common when people are competitive—wanting to win.
>
> - When Jasper's brother bought an expensive car, Jasper got a *more*-expensive car. Their one-upmanship is crazy.

36.

go one better *v. phr.*

To outdo someone (a little), to do even better or more than someone else has. This phrase was originally used in gambling, meaning to offer an even higher wager. Related: *one-upmanship*. This term refers to people wanting to prove they are better than someone else. *One up* means being a step ahead in a competition.

- Peter donated a hundred dollars to the charity, and Helen, per usual, had to go one better. She donated a hundred and fifty.
- I'm tired of his constant one-upmanship—always having to be better than his colleagues.

37.

all one *phr.*

(1) Considered the same, with no difference. (2) Of no importance (to a person). This phrase goes back to Old English (before 1066).

- Whether students tried hard or not doesn't matter to our professor. It's all one to him if they do poorly on tests.
- Hal doesn't care if we eat out or have dinner at home on his birthday; it's all one to him.

38.
one and the same *phr.*

The same, alike. This expression is stronger than just *the same*.

- The two companies have different names, but considering the way they operate, they are one and the same.
- Her grandfather was at one and the same time a doctor and an army officer.

39.
rolled up in one *phr.*

Two or more things or occupations combined into one. From at least 1797: "Will was so fat he appeared like a ton;—Or like two single gentlemen roll'd into One."

- The mall is a shopping center and children's amusement park rolled into one.
- Sherry is an accountant and sales manager rolled into one.

UNIQUE

40.
one of a kind *adj. phr., n. phr.*

Unique, rare, unlike any others. Usually spelled with hyphens when used as an adjective. Compare this idiom with *two of a kind* and *two peas in a pod* (p. 51).

- This novel is truly unique; it's a one-of-a-kind book.
- Mike will be hard to replace when he leaves the company; he's really one of a kind.

41.
the one and only *n. phr.*

(1) Used before the name of a unique or famous person. (2) Sweetheart or true love, sometimes spelled with hyphens: one-and-only.

- Ladies and gentlemen, I introduce to you the one and only Art Tatum, the most outstanding jazz pianist ever.
- Eunice said she's finally found her one-and-only.

42.

one for the road *n. phr.*

A final drink before leaving or going home. More than one dictionary has noted that the idea in this idiom is not a good one if the person is going to drive a car. Colloquial.

- How about one for the road?
- One for the road, and then I'm going to find a taxi.

43.

(all) in one piece *adv. phr.*

Not hurt or damaged. This idiom pictures something not breaking into pieces when there are problems.

- My car broke down twice, but I made it here in one piece.
- The furniture we shipped home arrived all in one piece.

SPORTS IDIOMS

44.

hole in one *n. phr.*

A perfect or great achievement. This idiom comes from golf, where it means hitting a ball from the tee (the start) and into the hole in a single stroke. In time it was used figuratively to mean "great success" with anything. The phrase is therefore like *home run*, which started in baseball and became used widely for "success."

- Tiger Woods hit a hole in one in the golf tournament today.
- Vicky hit a home run (or *hole in one*) on her history exam.

45.

one for the books *n. phr.*

Something that is incredible or notable. Sometimes also with the singular, *book*. This expression originally referred to record books that people kept for sports, but in time became used figuratively.

- Tim was voted employee of the month three times in a row. That's one for the books.
- I've never seen so many mistakes. This exam is one for the books.

46.
in one ear and out the other *phr.*

Quickly forgotten or ignored. This idiom pictures advice or information leaving a person's head as quickly as it enters. Colloquial.

- The teacher begged her students to prepare for the exam, but with most of them it was in one ear and out the other.
- My advice to Ken went in one ear and right out the other.

47.
it takes one to know one *clause.*

The person who is criticizing someone does the same thing or has the same fault. Similar: *It takes a thief to catch a thief.*

- "She's a terrible driver!" "Yeah, well, it takes one to know one." (= so are you)
- Don't talk. It takes one to know one.

48.
wear more than one hat *v. phr.*

To have more than one job or role. Also: *wear (number) hats, wear another hat, wear many hats.* This idiom refers to hats worn by people of different occupations—but here for only one person.

- Store managers wear any number of hats. We manage employees, do marketing, and even wash windows if needed.
- Steve has been wearing several hats at his restaurant since his partner left.

49.
pull a fast one *v. phr.*

To fool or cheat someone, to take unfair advantage of someone. Also: *put over a fast one.* Colloquial/slang. Originally US. *Pull* here means "to perform / carry out," as in *pull an all-nighter.*

- Always research before buying a car, or the salespeople will pull a fast one on you.
- She lied on her job application. She tried to pull a fast one (on the company).

> **A Few Small Words.** Many idioms are made up of simple, un-interesting words but have much-wider meanings. Compare these three phrases that have few differences in words but big differences in meaning.
>
> - one of those things
> - one of those days
> - one of these days

50.

one of those things   *n. phr.*

Something that cannot be avoided or explained; a fact one cannot change, so one must accept it. This idiom goes back to at least the 1920s. Often with *just: just one of those things.*

- We all have to pay taxes. It's just one of those things.
- Yes, your math class is boring. But some classes are going to be boring—it's one of those things.

51.

one of those days   *n. phr.*

A day on which everything goes wrong. A bad day, a difficult day.

- I overslept, the coffeemaker wouldn't work, my car wouldn't start … It was one of those days.
- Jack is the star player on our baseball team, but unfortunately, he had one of those days.

52.

one of these days   *adv. phr.*

Someday soon or in the future. Also: *one day.* This idiom shows the speaker thinking about something happening.

- One of these days, I'm going to have to buy a new computer. This one's too slow.
- Betty came to work late again? One of these days, she's going to get into trouble.

53.

put/have all (one's) eggs in one basket v. phr.

To risk having all your money, resources, etc., in only one venture (business, etc.).

- You're going to invest in only one stock? It's not smart to put all your eggs in one basket.
- Right now our company is selling only one product. We have all our eggs in one basket.

Suck Eggs? *The Oxford English Dictionary* notes that the word *egg* is used in several proverbs and phrases, including *put all (one's) eggs in one basket, as safe as eggs,* and (yes, try not to laugh) *teach your grandmother to suck eggs,* which means "to offer advice to someone who is much more experienced." (As with many colloquial idioms, it's best for English students to learn the meanings of phrases but necessarily use them. This latter phrase is an example.)

54.

more than one way to skin a cat phr.

More than one method of reaching a goal. An older, British idiom was more ways of *killing* a cat. It's unclear why either refers to hurting cats. The phrase goes back to at least the mid-1800s.

- There must be some alternative—there has to be more than one way to skin a cat.
- We missed the train, but we can still drive. There's more than one way to skin a cat.

55.

one-man show n. phr.

A business or event that is managed by only one person. This idiom pictures a show with only one actor. It can be both good and bad. Also: *one-man band.*

- Ian's bakery is a one-man show—he wears many hats.
- It's not much of a company, really. In fact, it's just a one-man show.

Review and Practice

Test Your Memory

Choose the best answer.

1. The storm was bad, but everyone got to work safely, ___.
   A. rolled up in one
   B. in one piece
   C. at one

2. The used-car salesman tried to pull a fast one on us. He tried to ___.
   A. fool us
   B. make a quick sale
   C. give us a discount

3. If my company is a one-man show, how many hats do I wear?
   A. one hat
   B. two hats
   C. every hat

4. The café is one of a kind. It ___.
   A. is inexpensive
   B. serves a rare cuisine
   C. is unique

5. Our boss loved Kyle's sales plan. Kyle ___.
   A. pulled a fast one
   B. hit a hole in one
   C. rolled up in one

6. Everything's been going wrong today. It's been ___.
   A. one of these days
   B. one of those days
   C. one of those things

7. My cat always wants to eat. She has a ___.
   A. one-track mind
   B. one fell swoop
   C. hole in one

8. My plan failed, so it's ___.
   A. back to square one
   B. one for the road
   C. rolled up in one

Good or Bad

For each idiom, choose G for a good situation or B for a bad one. When finished see the explanation in the Answer Key.

1. A-one ___

2. one too many ___

3. all in one piece ___

4. pull a fast one ___

5. one of those days ___

6. at one (with) ___

7. hole in one ___

8. in one ear and out the other ___

Quick Thought

As quickly as you can, think of an idiom that can have the following meanings. When finished, check the Answer Key.

1. comfortable

2. start over

3. remarkable

4. all at once

5. safely

6. a big accomplishment

7. doesn't listen

8. top quality

Section 3

What's the difference between *one on one* and *one by one*? How about *one to one*? By changing the preposition we have different idioms and different meanings. Other idioms have similar words but very different meanings, as well. What is the difference between *first off, first thing,* and *in the first place*?

First off, have a look at the idioms below and underline phrases you don't know the meaning of. Second off, try to guess their meaning. What do you think *with one voice* means? Is it good or bad to be *one jump ahead*?

- with one voice
- one and all
- (have) one eye on
- one good turn deserves another
- one man's meat ...
- one by one
- one way or another
- one picture is worth ...
- if at first you don't succeed ...
- first off
- at first
- in the first place
- (at) first hand
- first and last
- first lady
- first come, first served
- get to first base
- with one arm tied behind ...
- one jump ahead
- one foot in the grave
- one-horse town
- one on one
- one in a million
- one of the boys
- if you've seen one ...
- first thing
- first and foremost
- from the first
- first things first
- at first glance
- first blood
- love at first sight
- not know the first thing about
- single out

Study the following pages until you get to the Review and Practice section on page 44. Then return to the list above to review idioms you underlined.

> **Adverbs + with:** *With* in many idioms creates adverb phrases that show how something is done. These include speak *with one voice*, listen *with interest*, go in *with our eyes open (aware)*, and welcome *with open arms*.

56.

with one voice *adv. phr.*

Unanimously, with agreement by all. This old idiom was used by Chaucer in a story around 1380.

- The City Council spoke against the proposal with one voice.
- Kelly's students spoke with one voice when they complained her exams were too hard.

57.

with one arm tied behind (one's) back *adv. phr.*

Easily, without difficulty. This idiom pictures someone proving he or she has a skill by performing it with only one hand. Also: *with one hand, with (one's) eyes closed, blindfolded* (to have a cloth over one's eyes). Colloquial.

- Computers aren't hard to assemble. Heck, I could assemble a computer with one hand tied behind my back.
- Kent told his friends he could play the game blindfolded.

58.

one and all *n. phr.*

Everybody. This idiom goes back to Middle English, in the 1400s.
- Carrie wanted her discovery to benefit one and all, not just make a few people rich.
- And a good night to one and all.

59.

one jump ahead *phr.*

One step in front of; prepared for what will happen.
- The thief always stayed one jump ahead of the police.
- Our company always manages to stay one jump ahead of the competition.

60.

(have) one eye on   *v. phr.*

With (one's) partial attention; often watching or paying attention to one thing or person while doing something else. Similar: *keep an eye on*.

- Mike was so excited about the party, he had one eye on the clock while working, all afternoon.
- The detective had one eye on the door as he questioned the people in the room.

61.

one foot in the grave   *phr.*

Near death; in very bad health. The meaning of this idiom is obvious. It was used as early as the 1400s. It is one of many idioms that use the word *grave*. Colloquial.

- "Hurry," the doctor said, "this patient has one foot in the grave."
- Ben only has a cold, but he looks like he has one foot in the grave.

62.

one good turn deserves another   *clause.*

An act of good or a favor should be returned. Similar phrases were in use by the 1400s. This proverb was recorded in 1550: "One good tourne askth an other" (old spellings). *Turn* is used to mean an action. Opposite: *One bad turn deserves another* (rare).

- You paid for lunch yesterday, so I'm paying today. One good turn deserves another.
- If Peter helped you, be sure to help him when he needs it. One good turn deserves another.

63.

one-horse town *n. phr.*

A small town or city, an unimportant place. This idiom was in use by the 1850s. The phrase pictures a small rural town where nothing important happens. And while people drive cars today, the idiom is still quite common.

- Is there anything to do on weekends in this one-horse town?
- Leslie dreamed of one day getting out of the one-horse town she grew up in and moving to the big city.

64.

one man's meat is another man's poison *clause.*

What is good for one person is bad for someone else. This old proverb was recorded by 1576.

- Tim loves to travel, but Fred prefers to rest on vacations. One man's meat is another's poison.
- Not everyone in the hospital liked the new digital medical records. One man's meat, another man's poison.

65.

one on one *adv. phr., adj. phr.*

Directly between two people. This idiom possibly comes from sports, where one player from each team interacts. It is also the name of a basketball (or other sport) game for just two people.

- Teachers meet with students one on one at the end of every term.
- I found one-on-one classes to be best for learning Spanish.

66.

one by one *adv. phr.*

Separately, individually. One person or thing and then the next. Also: *one at a time.*

- One by one the students stopped by the professor's desk to thank her for a great semester.
- Our company carefully inspects all our products, one by one, to make sure they're good quality.

> *On, by, in,* and *to* ...
> - one on one = a two-person basketball game
> - one on one = one person for one person
> - two on one = two people for one person
> - one by one = one person or thing at a time
> - two by two = two people or things at a time
> - one to one = one person with one person
> - two in one = two uses for one machine
> - two to one = 66.6% to 33.3% chance/odds
> - three to one = 75% to 25% chance/odds
> - four to one, etc.

67.

one in a million   *n. phr.*

Very rare; special and unique. Sometimes *one in a thousand/billion/trillion*, though *million* is most common.

- George was a great manager; he succeeded by helping everyone succeed. He was one in a million.
- When it came to being a good husband, Marty was one in a million.

68.

one way or another   *adv. phr.*

Somehow, by some method. Also: *one way or the other.*

- I don't know where Tim is, but one way or another we have to find him.
- Carla didn't know how to fix her car, but she knew that one way or the other, she would.

69.

one of the boys   *n. phr.*

Accepted by a group of male friends.

- Mike finally became one of the boys when he joined the school's baseball team.
- Ned never felt like he was one of the boys.

70.

one picture is worth a thousand words *clause.*

You can learn a lot more from a picture than you can learn from an explanation; pictures are more effective than just words.

- Christie wants to become a photojournalist, because photos are what interest people in news stories. A picture is worth a thousand words.
- I'm all about images. You know what they say: A picture is worth a thousand words.

> **Story:** The saying "A picture is worth a thousand words" started as an advertising slogan in 1921, one used by an ad agency. The agency said the proverb was Japanese philosophy. In 1924, it changed the slogan to "The picture is worth ten thousand words," which the agency said was a Chinese proverb. Neither was Asian, though the use of "ten thousand" as a huge number is a feature of Chinese.

71.

If you've seen one, you've seen them all *clause.*

One example is enough; one doesn't need to see any more. Sometimes just *seen one, seen them all*. Also, a newer idiom similar in meaning: *Been there, done that.*

- So the movie has a big car chase? I don't care. If you've seen one, you've seen them all.
- Thanks, but I don't want to spend my day standing in lines at an amusement park. Been there, done that.

Idioms in the News

✎ "Acupuncture works, **one way or another**."
—CNN, Sept. 11, 2012.

✎ "Photos reveal how Las Vegas transformed from a **one-horse town** to the glitzy City of Lights."
—Daily Mail, July 30, 2015.

— First —

Ordinal numbers (*first, second, third* ...) make their way into idioms just as cardinal numbers (*one, two, three* ...) do. Many idioms with the word *first* serve as adverbs (see below). *First* can be an adjective (first person to arrive), an adverb (do this first), a noun (I was the first), and even a verb (first a legislative motion).

72.
if at first you don't succeed, try, try again   *clause.*

This proverb teaches that people should continue trying if they are not successful on the first try. The meaning is "Don't give up, don't quit." It goes back to at least 1840, when it was recorded in a teacher's manual: " 'T is a lesson you should heed, Try, try again; If at first you don't succeed, Try, try again." Today this saying is often shortened to just *if at first you don't succeed* ...

- It's too bad I didn't get the job. But you know what they say: If at first you don't succeed ...
- That didn't fix the computer. Oh, well, try, try again.

ADVERBS

> **Adverbs:** Many idioms with *first* serve as adverbs or sentence adverbs. These include *first thing, first off, first and foremost, at first, from the first, in the first place, (at) first hand, at first glance,* and *first and last.*

73.
first thing   *adv. phr.*

Before doing other tasks, as early as possible. *Thing* here means "matter" or "task." See also: *first off* and *first things first* (below).

- Be sure to write the report first thing tomorrow morning. It's urgent.
- I'll text you first thing after I arrive.

74.

first off *adv. phr.*

In the beginning, before others. Also: *first of all, firstly, first.* Compare: *second of all, secondly, third of all,* etc. See also: *first and foremost* (below).

- Why don't I want to go swimming? Well, first of all, it's freezing outside. Second of all ...
- First of all, clean the kitchen. Then take out the garbage.

75.

first and foremost *adv. phr.*

(1) Most importantly. (2) To begin with. See also: *first off, first thing,* and *first and foremost.* From at least the 1500s.

- Carl's bio says he is first and foremost a reporter.
- We have many things to talk about today, but first and foremost, we need to make a schedule.

76.

at first *adv. phr.*

Early on, originally. This expression is used to show how an experience or action changed, how it was different later.

- At first Brenda loved living in a big city, but soon the noise and pollution began to bother her.
- I liked this restaurant at first, but it's gone downhill (become bad).

77.

from the first *adv. phr.*

Ever since something started, from the beginning.

- From the first Tina didn't like the hotel.
- I thought the new teacher was good from the first.

Idioms in the News

✎ "Advertisers Need to Be Storytellers—**First and Foremost**"
—Wall Street Journal, June 20, 2016.

78.

in the first place *adv. phr.*

(1) In the beginning, before other things were said or done. (2) The most important of several reasons or arguments.

- You don't need this computer today? Why didn't you tell me that in the first place. I just spent twenty minutes trying to fix it.
- Why can't we have Chinese food for dinner? Well, in the first place, the restaurant is very expensive.

79.

first things first *phr.*

(To deal with) the most-important matter before others. This phrase means "Let's look at what is really important before we look at other matters."

- Yes, there are hundreds of places we want to see here in New York, but first things first: Let's find a hotel.
- "First things first" is my policy for meetings at work.

80.

(at) first hand *adv. phr., adj.phr.*

Directly from a source, without someone else in between. This phrase is used with verbs such as *know, hear, see* and *learn*. When not used with "at," the phrase is often hyphenated (first-hand) or closed (firsthand). It is also a common adjective (first-hand knowledge, firsthand account). Opposite: *secondhand*.

- I've seen firsthand how big of a problem crime is in big cities.
- The reporter wanted to hear at first hand what witnesses saw. A secondhand account was not good enough.

81.

at first glance *adv. phr.*

When first seen. This idiom shows how something appeared when first seen or considered. Also: a*t first blush, at first sight.*

- At first glance, I knew Jenkins was going to be a hard worker.
- At first glance, we liked the house, but as we explored, we discovered many problems.

82.

first and last *adv. phr.*

Under all circumstances, overall. This idiom from the 1300s meant "from start to finish" and the 1500s "overall." Similar: *above all.*

- Whether or not you should wear a bicycle helmet is first and last a matter of safety.
- Her goal first and last was to improve her students' knowledge.

83.

first blood *n. phr.*

The first advantage gained or damage done in a contest. Often used with the verb *draw*. This idiom comes from war, when it meant the first killing/wounding. Today it is used widely in sports.

- Our baseball team drew first blood, scoring a run only minutes into the game.
- The two salesmen are having a contest to see who can sell the most cars in one day. Let's see who draws first blood.

84.

first lady *n. phr.*

The wife of a president, prime minister, or head of a country (or province, state, city, etc.). Also: *first family, first son/daughter,* and even *first dog,* a president's pet. These terms are sometimes capitalized, though First Dog may be capitalized for humor.

- The president and the first lady hosted a dinner for the visiting prime minister.
- The prime minister was often seen walking the First Dog.

85.

love at first sight *n. phr.*

The act of falling in love with someone or something when first seeing it. This idiom was used by the 1300s (Chaucer). Nowadays people use it for things as well as people.

- The moment he saw her, he knew it was love at first sight.
- Mark didn't need to test-drive the car. He knew immediately it was the car for him. It was love at first sight.

86.
first come, first served *phr.*

This common phrase is used to tell customers that people will be helped or served in the order that they arrive (e.g., at a restaurant).

- The sign says, "First come, first served," and considering how long the line is, we're going to be here all afternoon.
- Seats on the train were given on a first-come-first-served basis.

87.
not know the first thing about *v. phr.*

To have no knowledge (or ability) about a subject. *First thing* here means "most basic." Also: *not know beans about*. US, colloquial.

- Tim is a great professor, but he doesn't know the first thing about how to use a computer.
- Tammy doesn't know beans about how to cook.

88.
get to first base *v. phr.*

To succeed in the beginning. Also: *reach first base*. This common sports idiom comes from baseball. To score, players must hit a ball and run around three bases to a fourth, called home plate. With a small hit, players can run to first base. With a bad hit, they can't get even that far. This idiom is used figuratively, outside the sport.

- Kim hopes to get hired as a teacher at the school, and she's made it to first base: She has an interview tomorrow.
- Our company tried to open a second office, but we didn't even get to first base. We couldn't find a good building.

89.
single out *phrasal verb.*

To choose or distinguish someone or something. By the 1500s, *single* was used as a verb by itself, meaning "to separate." Today *out* is added. Compare with *pick out* (select).

- I don't know why the professor singled me out to answer the question.
- Stacy's manager singled her out for a promotion.

Review and Practice

Test Your Memory

Choose the best answer.

1. ___, I didn't understand, but once the teacher explained, I got it.
   A. at first
   B. first thing
   C. first place

2. Teaching is more important to me than publishing; I am ___ a teacher.
   A. first thing
   B. first and last
   C. at first

3. The teacher met with each student individually; they met ___.
   A. one up one
   B. one on one
   C. one at one

4. Enter one at a time, or ___.
   A. one on one
   B. one to one
   C. one by one

5. Images are very important in books. One picture is ___.
   A. at first glance
   B. one good turn
   C. worth a thousand words

6. Our company is always ___ of other companies; we always beat them.
   A. one good turn
   B. one jump ahead
   C. one in a million

7. We will succeed somehow. We'll find a way. We'll succeed ___.
   A. first and foremost
   B. on first base
   C. one way or another

8. We had a bad start. We didn't ___.
   A. get first served
   B. get to first base
   C. get to first sight

Good or Bad

For each idiom, choose G for a good situation or B for a bad one. When finished, see the explanation in the Answer Key.

1. love at first sight ___

2. one arm tied behind (one's) back ___

3. one jump ahead ___

4. one foot in the grave ___

5. (teach) one on one ___

6. one in a million ___

7. one of the boys ___

8. not get to first base ___

Quick Thought

As quickly as you can, think of an idiom that can have the following meanings. When finished, check the Answer Key.

1. (do) with agreement

2. everyone

3. individually

4. personally

5. unique

6. not worth seeing

7. accepted, friendly with others

8. very ill

Section 4

Numerous idioms with the word *once* are adverb phrases or sentence adverbs, phrases like *once in a while, once in a blue moon, once in a lifetime,* and *once and for all.*

Two appears in many idioms. What does it mean if I have *two left feet*? Is it bad if a person is *two-faced*? And if *it takes two to tango*, what do you do if you have *two left feet*?

Take a look at the idioms below. Underline phrases you don't know. Then try to guess their meanings. Look at their words and try to *put two and two together*.

- once upon a time
- once in a blue moon
- once in a lifetime
- once and for all
- stand on (one's) own two feet
- Goody Two-shoes
- two heads are better than one
- two and two make four
- it takes two to tango
- two's company, three's a crowd
- know a thing or two
- no two ways about it
- cut two/both ways
- that makes two of us
- for two cents
- two strikes against (one)

- (every) once in a while
- all at once
- give (someone) the once-over
- Fool me once, shame on you ...
- have two left feet
- two-faced
- put two and two together
- two wrongs don't make a right
- two can play at that game
- two of a kind
- tell (someone) a thing or two
- two-way street
- of two minds
- two bits
- (one's) two cents' worth
- kill two birds with one stone

Study the following pages until you get to the Review and Practice section on page 56. Then return to the list above to review idioms you underlined.

— Once —

Once can be an adverb, a conjunction, an adjective, and a noun. And *once in a while* you will come across *once* in an idiom.

ADVERB PHRASES

90.
once upon a time *adv. phr.*

At some point or time in the past. This phrase is often used to begin fairy tales. It goes back to at least the 1590s and before that was written as *once on a time*.

- Yeah, once upon a time I could have lifted all these boxes by myself, but my days of heavy lifting are over. I'm too old.
- Once upon a time, there were three bears …

91.
(every) once and a while *adv. phr.*

Occasionally. Also: *every now and then, from time to time*.

- Every once in a while Sandy goes out to an expensive restaurant all by herself and enjoys a good—and quiet—meal.
- I like to have guests over for tea once in a while. And dinner, too, every now and then.

92.
once in a blue moon *adv. phr.*

Rarely, very rarely. A blue moon is a second full moon in a calendar month. They are not blue in color, though. The moon might appear blue in color at any time.

- It never snows where I live, but once in a blue moon we get snow in the nearby mountains.
- Once in a blue moon I make curry.

93.
all at once *adv. phr.*

(1) At the same time. (2) Suddenly, when unexpected.

- We can't take a lunch break all at once, so you guys eat first.
- All at once the rain stopped and the sky turned blue.

94.

once in a lifetime   *adv. phr., adj. phr.*

Very rarely, maybe never again. Also used as an adjective: *once-in-a-lifetime*. The phrase was recorded by the 1850s.

- The chance to marry someone you truly love may come only once in a lifetime.
- Clarence felt the job offer was a once-in-a-lifetime opportunity.

95.

give (someone/something) the once-over   *v. phr.*

To look at someone briefly to assess or judge what the person is like. Also used for things.

- The first time I met our company's president, she gave me a quick once-over before shaking my hand.
- The chef personally gave the table a once-over to make sure everything was perfect, before the guests arrived.

96.

once and for all   *adv. phr.*

Completely, finally. An older form, *once for all,* dates from the 1400s.

- The two managers decided to sit down and settle their differences once and for all.
- We wish our professor would decide once and for all whether there's going to be a final exam. She keeps changing her mind.

97.

Fool me once, shame on you; fool me twice, shame on me.

This proverb means one should learn one's lesson the first time, and not be fooled a second time. Note that *fool* is used as a verb, meaning "to trick" or "to deceive." Sometimes also: *Fool me once, shame on thee; fool me twice, shame on me*, so that *thee* (you) rhymes with *me*. Often shortened to just *fool me once* ...

- I believed you once before. Sorry, but you know the saying: "Fool me once ..."
- I won't fall for (be tricked by) that again. "Fool me once" and all that.

— Two —

The modern English *two* developed sometime before 1200 AD from the Old English *twá* (725 AD). The word is similar in several Indo-European languages, ranging from Sanskrit *dwau/dwē* to Latin *duo* to Old Irish *dá* to Lithuanian *du/dvi*.

Here we'll see the many idioms made with the word *two*.

PARTS OF THE BODY

98.

stand on (one's) own two feet *v. phr.*

To be independent, to be able to take care of oneself. This idiom refers to not needing help to stand up.

- I don't need financial help. I can stand on my own two feet.
- Cheryl knew she needed to stand on her own two feet for once, and not ask friends for help.

99.

have two left feet *v. phr.*

To be unable to dance, to be a poor dancer. This idiom pictures feet that cannot work together, that cannot coordinate. It originally meant "clumsy," but by 1915 was used for dancing. From 1857: "... born with two left hands and two left feet." Colloquial.

- I'll never learn this dance. I simply have two left feet.
- Jane went to the party, but stayed off the dance floor saying she had two left feet.

100.

Goody Two-shoes *n. phr.*

A person who always follows the rules, who is prude, thinking he or she is better than others. From a 1765 fairy tale. Colloquial.

- Stop being a Goody Two-shoes.
- Well, look at Goody Two-shoes over here, afraid to break rules.

101.
two-faced *adj. phr.*

Deceitful, untrustworthy. This idiom describes someone who says one thing to some people but another to others. Colloquial.

- Jill always tells Carl she's his best friend, but she says bad things about him to others. She's really two-faced.
- That's not what you said to Bill. Don't be two-faced.

102.
two heads are better than one *clause.*

Two people can do a job better than one person; cooperation is better. This old idiom from the 1500s is still common today, in business English and everyday English. It is especially appropriate for jobs that require thinking.

- "Jake, I could use your help." "No problem. Two heads are better than one."
- Paul wrote plans for the book and did research, and Randy did most of the writing. They figured two heads were better than one.

MATH

103.
put two and two together *v. phr.*

To figure something out, to understand what really happened.

- It didn't take long for the police to put two and two together, and they soon arrested the robber.
- You know he'll put two and two together before too long.

104.
two and two make four *clause.*

An obvious conclusion, something that is easy to see and understand. This phrase obviously pictures simple math.

- The economy will get better if we lower taxes—it's as simple as two and two make four.
- Next you're going to tell me two and two make five.

105.
two wrongs don't make a right *clause.*

A second wrongful action will not make a first one better. This idiom was recorded as a proverb in 1768 ("Two wrongs will not make one right"). A similar phrase, "two wrongs infer one right," appeared in *The London Magazine* in 1734.

- You shouldn't take someone else's umbrella just because someone took yours. Two wrongs don't make a right.
- Perhaps two wrongs don't make a right, but five hundred wrongs positively must make a right. (From a 1922 novel.)

TWO PEOPLE

106.
it takes two to tango *clause.*

Two people must act to make something successful, not just one. Both people are responsible. The tango is a dance that became popular in the 1920s. It requires two dancers to both move in certain ways. Here, the name of the dance, *tango*, is used as a verb. This idiom became widely known in the 1950s from the song "Takes Two to Tango," which was recorded by Pearl Bailey in 1952 (listen to the recording on YouTube). See also: *two-way street* (below).

- If our manager wants us to work overtime, we should at least get overtime pay. It takes two to tango.
- Remember, to have a successful marriage, both the husband and the wife must work hard. It takes two to tango.

107.
two can play at that game *clause.*

Others can act in the same way or do the same thing. This idiom is often used as a threat, to state that one is ready to respond in the same way. Also: *That's a game that two can play.* Colloquial.

- He won't to talk to me? Well, two can play at that game. I won't talk to him, either.
- Mike refused to load paper in the office printer, so I refused, too. It was a game two could play.

108.
two's company, three's a crowd *clause.*

A third person spoils a romantic time. This proverb goes back to at least the 1600s. Often shortened to just *two's company* or *three's a crowd*. Also: *Two's company, three's none.*

- Thanks for inviting me to join you and Hank for dinner, but tomorrow's Valentine's Day. Three's a crowd.
- Do you have a table for two, where we can dine in privacy. Two's company, more's none, after all.

109.
two of a kind *n. phr.*

Very similar, for people or things. Compare: *one of a kind* ("unique," above). Also: *like two peas in a pod.*

- Jasper and Frank are two of a kind. They both spend all their free time playing video games.
- After thirty years' marriage, they were like two peas in a pod.

KNOWLEDGE

110.
know a thing or two *v. phr.*

To be very experienced or knowledgeable about something. This and similar phrases have been in use since at least the 1600s. Also: *know all the answers, know (one's) way around, know a trick or two.* Colloquial.

- Penny's the person to go to for advice on buying a new laptop. She knows a thing or two about computers.
- I can help you learn to cook. I know my way around a kitchen.

111.
tell (someone) a thing or two *v. phr.*

(1) To tell someone about something. (2) To tell someone why you are angry or what someone has done wrong. Colloquial.

- Penny told me a thing or two about how to buy a new computer.
- I told the manager a thing or two about the poor service!

112.

no two ways about it *phr.*

Definitely true. Used to show something cannot be argued with. *Ways* here means "outlooks"or "plans."

- We need a new car! There's no two ways about it. Our old car just isn't safe.
- That was the best concert I've ever been to. There's no two ways about it.

113.

two-way street *n. phr.*

A situation that requires both people to act. This idiom refers to a street having cars going in both directions. It is similar to *It takes two to tango* (above).

- Love is a two-way street. Both people have to work hard.
- Managing employees is a two-way street. The manager must care for the employees, just as they work for the manager.

> **Streets:** A *one-way street* is a road that allows traffic in only one direction, often so that more cars can pass faster. While this sounds like something new for cars, the first one-way streets were introduced in London in 1616, on alleys near the River Thames. Paris got its first one-way streets in 1909, one of them Place Charles de Gaulle around the Arc de Triomphe.

114.

cut two/both ways *v. phr.*

To have both good and bad results. This idiom refers to a *double-edged sword*, which is sharp on both sides. Similar idioms are *two-edged sword* and *double-edged sword*.

- Our company's high prices cut both ways: We sell fewer products, but we are known for quality.
- Take-home exams are a two-edged sword. They're less stressful but students have to work much harder.

115.

of two minds *adj. phr.*

Undecided, often between two choices. Today the idiom is usually *of two minds*, though in the past was *of diverse minds* (1500s on), *of many/several minds, of twenty minds.*

- Lisa is of two minds about her new apartment. She thinks it's small, but it's in a great location, next to a night market.
- I'm still of two minds on whether or not to take the job.

116.

that makes two of us *clause.*

One agrees; one also feels this way. *Make* here means "add up to" or "equal" as in *two plus two makes four.*

- "I'm ready for lunch." "That makes two of us."
- Ronny told me he is worried about our company, and that makes two of us.

MONEY

117.

two bits / two-bit *n. phr., adj. phr.*

(1) *Two bits* is an American term for 25 cents. (2) *Two-bit* means "cheap," "low-quality." (Similar: *for two cents,* below.)

- Ah, I remember when a can of soda cost only two bits. Today two bits won't buy you anything.
- Ted didn't want to stay at a two-bit hotel.

118.

for two cents *adv. phr.*

(1) For nothing; in exchange for a small amount of money. (2) Not valuable, not worth much. *Two cents* probably comes from the British *twopence,* which is a sum of two pennies, and also a coin worth that amount.

- For two cents I would quit this job!
- Kim's rich, famous friends made her feel like two cents.

119.

(one's) two cents' worth *n. phr.*

A person's opinion. Often *put in (one's) two cents*, meaning "to give one's opinion." Sometimes also just *(one's) two cents* (see below).

- Jill put in her two cents and left the meeting.
- There. That's my two cents' worth for you. That's my opinion.

121.

two strikes against (one) *n. phr.*

Already in trouble, often for two things. This idiom comes from baseball, where players have three tries to hit a well-thrown ball. When players fail to hit a well-thrown ball, it's called a *strike*. If they have two strikes, they know their next strike means they are *out* (it will be another player's turn). This idiom has long been used figuratively, outside of baseball. See also: *three strikes* (below).

- Helen often comes to work late and she doesn't have management experience, so in the race to become our new manager, she has two strikes against her.
- Ned dared not make a mistake at work, knowing he already had two strikes against him.

122.

kill two birds with one stone *v. phr.*

To do two things with one action, to accomplish two things at once. This well-known idiom is often shortened to just *kill two birds*. It goes back to at least the 1600s.

- Henry was able to kill two birds with one stone when he hired Jean—she's both an experienced manager and an accountant.
- I hoped to kill two or three birds with a single trip to the mall.

PETA, the animal rights group, wants people to stop using idioms that refer to harming animals. So instead of *kill two birds with one stone,* they want people to say *feed two birds with one scone.* It's a noble effort, but attempts to change a language this way are rarely successful.

Crossword Puzzle

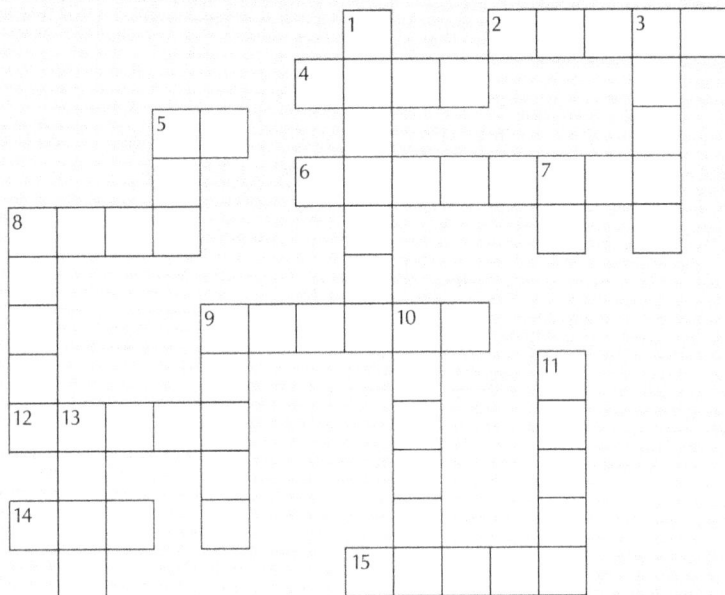

ACROSS

2. I believe holding the meeting outdoors is a mistake. That's my two ___.

4. There is no other restaurant like it. It is truly one of a ___.

5. The customers entered the store one at a time. They entered one ___ one.

6. Jill hates spending money, so she eats out only once in a ___.

8. Hank can't dance at all. He has two left ___.

9. There's nothing we can do about the rain. It's just one of those ___.

12. Everything has gone wrong today. It's really been one of ___ days.

14. The employees all agreed. They spoke with ___ voice.

15. Yes, you can help me plan. Two ___ are better than one.

DOWN

1. The professor's students love her. They say she is one in a ___.

3. I'll make the telephone call as soon as I get to work tomorrow. I'll do it first ___ in the morning.

5. Pete didn't want to stay at some two-___ hotel. He wanted a nice one.

7. The teacher met the students separately. He met them one ___ one.

8. Terry instantly loved the car; it was love at ___ sight.

9. One of ___ days, I'm going to buy a new computer.

10. At first ___ I thought she was my teacher, but then I saw she wasn't.

11. I can't decide whether to take the new job. I am of two ___.

12. I saw it myself. I saw it at first ___.

Review and Practice

Test Your Memory

Choose the best answer.

1. You keep changing your mind. Please decide ___ what you want to do.
   - A. once upon a time
   - B. once and for all
   - C. all at once

2. The job offer was a once-in-a-lifetime opportunity. It was ___.
   - A. quite common
   - B. very kind
   - C. extremely rare

3. If Donny is two-faced, you know you ___.
   - A. can't trust him
   - B. have a good diplomat
   - C. have protection

4. I think we should go. That's my ___.
   - A. two minds
   - B. two cents
   - C. two bits

5. I gave the coat the ___ before I bought it, to see if it was damaged.
   - A. all at once
   - B. once-over
   - C. once and for all

6. Kim thinks it is too hot to work? So do I, so that ___. I agree.
   - A. makes two of us
   - B. takes two to tango
   - C. makes it a two-way street

7. Tim didn't have a lot of money, so he had to stay in a ___ hotel.
   - A. two-cent
   - B. two-mind
   - C. two-bit

8. I am certain. There's no ___ it.
   - A. two ways about
   - B. two minds about
   - C. two bits about

Good or Bad

For each idiom, choose G for a good situation or B for a bad one. When finished see the Answer Key.

1. stand on (one's) own two feet ___

2. two's company ___

3. two strikes against (one) ___

4. fool (someone) ___

5. two-faced ___

6. two wrongs ___

7. two left feet ___

8. of two minds ___

Quick Thought

As quickly as you can, think of an idiom that has the following meanings. When finished, check the Answer Key.

1. person who follows rules

2. figure out

3. extremely rare

4. I agree

5. my opinion

6. twenty-five cents

7. already in trouble

8. can't dance

Section 5

The words *second, twice,* and *double* show up in numerous idioms. For example, no one wants to play *second fiddle*, have *second best*, or travel *second class*. And while *lightning never strikes twice in the same spot*, people do sometimes get a *double whammy*.

Look at the idioms below. Underline phrases you don't know. Then try to guess their meanings. Look at the words they contain and try to figure out their meanings.

- second nature
- second cousin
- second childhood
- second hand
- second class
- a close second
- have second thoughts
- second-guess
- once bitten, twice shy
- lightning never strikes in ...
- double date
- double whammy
- double standard
- double back
- double up
- on the double
- lead a double life

- second fiddle
- second wind
- second honeymoon
- second best
- second to none
- (on) second thought
- not give a second thought
- once or twice
- think twice
- double cross
- double duty
- double feature
- double-talk
- double over
- see double
- do a double take

Study the following pages until you get to the Review and Practice section on page 70. Then return to the list above to review idioms you underlined.

— Second —

Second can be an adjective, as in *second choice* and *second cup of tea*; a noun as in *the second in line* or *second in a race*; an adverb as in *second largest city* and *come in second in a race*; and a verb, meaning to be the second person to support a proposal.

The word certainly finds its way into many idioms.

SECOND + NOUN

123.
second nature   *n. phr.*

Ability to do something easily, without thinking, often because it's something you've done a lot. From an old proverb, *Habit is second nature,* which goes back to Latin and ancient Greek.

- Driving on San Francisco's steep, crowded streets was second nature to Laura. She'd grown up in the city.
- After ten years in the classroom, Don found that entertaining people came second nature to him.

124.
second fiddle   *n. phr.*

One who has a supporting role, one whose role is less important. Often with *play*: *play second fiddle.* A *fiddle* is a violin. See below.

- Ben hated playing second fiddle to his older brother.
- After hiring a new president, our CEO stepped back and played second fiddle in day-to-day business.

> **Note:** Bands and orchestras have *sections* (violin section, trumpet section, etc.). Sections then have a *first chair,* a *second chair,* etc. The first chair often plays the hardest part, while the second and third chairs play supporting parts. A person who *plays second fiddle* plays the second (chair) violin part.

125.

second cousin   *n. phr.*

(1) A child of a parent's first cousin (e.g., mother's cousin's son).
(2) Something that is similar or related but not the same.

- Eric is second cousin to Rita. They are second cousins.
- This band's music is considered second cousin to the music of the Beatles.

126.

second wind   *n. phr.*

A new feeling of energy after becoming tired, so that one can continue working or doing something. This idiom, which goes back to the early 1800s, comes from sports, where it means to begin breathing regularly after being out of breath. It is often used with *catch* or *get*.

- Pete was falling behind in the race, but he caught a second wind and won.
- Take a break and have a cup of coffee. Maybe you'll get a second wind.

127.

second childhood   *n. phr.*

(1) A period when an elderly person begins feeling young again. A period when an elderly person is playful and no longer has to work.
(2) A period when an elderly person loses mental ability.

- My father entered a second childhood the moment he got a sports car.
- Jenna needs a lot of care now that she's in her second childhood, so she's moving into a retirement home.

Idioms in the News

- ✎ "Rosamund Pike says actors won't 'play **second fiddle**' to actresses." (Rosamund Pike, an actress, says male actors don't want to be less important than female actors.)
  —BBC News, June 4, 2018.

128.

second honeymoon *n. phr.*

A trip or vacation like a honeymoon but taken after a couple has been married for some years. This phrase goes back to the 1800s.

- Amy and Bill are taking a second honeymoon next month.
- For years, my parents have been planning to go on a second honeymoon after they both retire.

129.

second hand *adv. phr., adj.*

(1) Used, owned by someone before. With this meaning the term today is often spelled as one word in American English: *secondhand*. (2) Through a second person. With this meaning the term is sometimes *at second hand*. (3) A hand on a clock that counts seconds. This phrase goes back to at least the 1400s.

- This is a secondhand car. I bought it secondhand.
- We heard the news secondhand (at second hand).

Used: "Used" sounds less than best. The term *used car* is what most people say (used-car dealer, ~ salesman). But car dealers use the term *pre-owned,* which means "owned before." It sounds nicer. Likewise, look for a used computer on the Internet and you'll find instead the term *refurbished,* meaning "used but fixed up." Again, it sounds nicer.

BEST OR LESS

130.

second best *n. phr., adj. phr.*

(1) Inferior in quality; not the best. (2) Number two in quality or in a competition, as in *best, second best, third best*, etc.

- Wendy's father told her she should never settle for second best in life.
- In our company, we are not satisfied with being second best; we always work to be the best.

second class *n. phr., adj. phr., adv. phr.*

Inferior in quality or service (hotels, trains, etc.) As an adjective, often hyphenated. Also: *second-rate*. Compare with *first-class*.

- We stayed at a second-class hotel. It was really second-rate.
- Hank hates spending money. He always travels second class.

> **Class:** *Second class* sounds unpleasant, so airlines especially invent new words for the different "classes"or levels of travel service. Most airlines offer *first class, business class,* and *economy class* (or *coach*). Many have used brand names for business class, such as *Clipper Class, Envoy,* and *Magnifica*.

second to none *phr.*

The best. Better than others. Often used to describe foods, services, hotels, etc. This idiom was used by Shakespeare in 1616.

- Kevin promised us the restaurant's sushi was second to none, and he was quite correct.
- Both manufacturers claim their factories and products are second to none.

a close second *n. phr.*

(1) Nearly as good as the best. (2) A number two winner in a race or competition who nearly wins. From 1823: "Mr. Thompson kept a close second to Mr. Thompson in the 5th mile."

- This smartphone is the best, but yours is a close second.
- Matt won the race, but Vicky came in a close second.

Idioms in the News

- "In Sports, Boston Is Now **Second to None**." (The city of Boston has several professional sports teams.)
  —The New York Times, April 13, 2017.

THINKING

134.

(on) second thought   *adv. phr.*

After considering something a second time, changing one's mind. Sometimes plural, *thoughts*. From 1581: "I finde verified the Prouerbe, That the second thoughtes are euer the best (I find true the proverb that second thoughts are best)" (old spellings).

- Let's eat out tonight! No, wait, we need to save money. On second thought, let's eat in.
- You can probably finish the job yourself, but if on second thought you feel you need help, let me know.

135.

have second thoughts   *v. phr.*

To become uncertain about a plan or decision one has made, to become unsure if it is a good idea. Also: *get cold feet*.

- Mark's been having second thoughts about taking the new job. He's worried the pay is too low.
- Phillip knew that the morning of his wedding was a very bad time to get cold feet about marriage, but he was scared.

136.

not give a second thought   *v. phr.*

To not worry about something. The idea is one will not worry (have a second thought) about something, or one wants someone not to worry. See also: *think twice* (below), *have second thoughts* (above).

- I'll help you fix your computer after work. And don't give it a second thought—I don't mind. I like working on computers.
- Kim told Don not to give a second thought to the broken vase.

Idioms in the News

✎ "**On second thought**: Maybe smartphones make us 'SuperStupid'?" (Opinion asking whether *smart*phones make people stupid. *Super stupid* means "very stupid.")
—CNN.com, Sept. 12, 2012.

137.

second-guess *v. phr.*

To question or criticize someone's decision, often after the result is known. Occasionally, this can be a positive action.

- Barry and Phil spend an hour after each football game second-guessing players' decisions.
- Can you look at my sales plan for next month? I need someone to second-guess me.

Second Look: This term *second-guess* likely comes from baseball, but lovers of all sports will understand. The term probably comes from *second-guesser*. These were people who criticized baseball players and umpires *after* a game. Such fans exist in every sport. Today people use the term *second-guess* figuratively, for anything.

Idioms in the News

✎ "150 years after Alaska sale, some Russians **have second thoughts**." (In 1867, the United States bought Alaska from Russia for $7.2 million, or 4.7 cents per hectare.)
—Seattle Times, March 30, 2017.

✎ "6 Questions That'll Make You **Second-Guess** Your Career Change Plans (In a Good Way!)" (Advice for young people on career plans.)
—Forbes, April 6, 2016.

✎ "Pizza still the focus at Domino's HQ, but tech **a close second**." (Technology at Domino's headquarters.)
—M Live (Michigan Live), June 29, 2017.

✎ "**Second Wind** for Michael Phelps, as a Swimmer and a Person." (Olympic swimmer Michael Phelps is back.)
—New York Times, April 19, 2015.

— Twice —

Once, twice, thrice ... Twice means "two times" or "on two occasions." Uses include *do something twice, twice absent, twice as much,* and *twice two is four.*

138.
once or twice *adv. phr.*

A few times. From at least the 1300s, including Chaucer.

- "Have you been to London?" "Yes, once or twice."
- Remember, when you're staying with your cousins, be sure to buy them dinner once or twice.

139.
once bitten, twice shy *phr.*

Someone will not repeat something after having a bad experience the first time. Note, the past participle of *bite* is *bit* or *bitten.*

- Sheila tried that restaurant and got sick. There's no way she'll go back. You know what they say: Once bitten, twice shy.
- I have been bit once, and have made a vow (promise) never to settle upon any woman while I live, again. (From a 1751 novel.)

140.
think twice *v. phr.*

To consider a decision or plan carefully; to reconsider it. This idiom is often used to warn people to think carefully or to warn of danger.

- Think twice before you invest money in that company.
- George should think twice about accepting the job offer.

141.
lightning never strikes twice in the same place *clause.*

Bad luck will not happen again. This idiom refers to the myth that lightning can't strike in the same place two times. Often shortened.

- I won't lose money this time. Lightning never strikes twice.
- Don't be afraid. Lightning never strikes in the same place twice.

— Double —

The word *double* as an adjective appears in terms such as *double room* (in a hotel) and *double digits* (10-99). As a verb, it appears in *The price doubled, I'll double my offer from fifty dollars to one hundred,* and *Mark doubles as a salesman and an accountant.* The word is also a noun, as in *She is my double in that company.* Importantly here, there are double the number of idioms using *double* as there are idioms using *twice.*

142.
double cross   *n. phr., v. phr.*

A betrayal, a failure to do something one promised. Also a verb: *double-cross.* This idiom comes from gambling and sports, where it meant "to pretend to cooperate and then betray someone." It was soon used figuratively, for dishonest transactions, etc.

* Sheila did not trust her business partner after his double cross.
* I promise I won't double-cross you.

143.
double date   *n. phr., v. phr.*

A *date,* such as dinner or a move, with two couples. Also a verb: *double-date.* This idiom goes back to at least the 1930s.

* Sherry has a new boyfriend. We should go on a double date.
* Mark and Fred are double dating with two classmates next weekend.

144.
double duty   *n. phr.*

Two roles, fulfilling two roles, for people or things. Often used with the verb *do.* One's *duty* is the job one must do.

* Our boss is on vacation this week, so I'm doing double duty as a manager and a salesman.
* George's truck does double duty as his work truck and his family car.

145.

double whammy *n. phr.*

Something that happens that is bad in two ways. This idiom was used in sports in the 1940s and in 1951 appeared in the comic strip "Li'l Abner." Also: *triple whammy.*

- For me the storm was a double whammy: I couldn't go to work and my house got flooded.
- The recession was a triple whammy for Ted.

146.

double feature *n. phr.*

Two movies or shows together, sometimes for the price of one. This idiom was originally used at movie theaters, but later television stations used the term for two films shown together. Also: *double bill.* A similar term used in sports is *doubleheader* (or *double-header*), which is two games (such as baseball) played together.

- The Main Street Cinema has a double feaure every Sunday afternoon.
- Our baseball team will play a doubleheader this weekend.

147.

double standard *n. phr.*

Unfair rules that treat some people differently than others.

- The president has a double standard on taxes: He wants to raise them for working people but lower them for the rich.
- Our school cannot be allowed to have a double standard on admissions, on who gets in and who doesn't.

148.

double-talk *n. phr.*

(1) Speech or language that has two possible meanings or that means nothing. (2) Speech or language that is made difficult to understand on purpose.

- I don't want to hear any more of your double-talk.
- All we got from Customer Service was a bunch of double-talk. They couldn't help us.

149.

double back *phrasal verb.*

To turn around and return in the direction in which one came.

- If we can't find the restaurant soon, we'll double back and see if we missed it.
- A tree had fallen in the road, so we had to double back.

150.

double over *phrasal verb.*

To bend forward suddenly because of pain, laughter, etc. Also: *double up.*

- We both doubled up laughing when we heard the joke.
- Marla doubled over in pain.

151.

double up *phrasal verb.*

To share, especially rooms, as in a hotel.

- To save money on hotel rooms, the students doubled up on the trip.
- The house has only three rooms and there are four of us, so two of us will have to double up.

152.

see double *v. phr.*

To see two images instead of one. Often caused by alcohol or medicine.

- Perry doesn't like wine. If he drinks even one glass, he'll be seeing double.
- Jill and her twin sister look so much alike, I thought I was seeing double.

Idioms in the News

✎ "The Insane **Double Standard** for Women Working in Tech."
—Inc.com, Aug. 28, 2014.

153.

on the double   *adv. phr.*

Immediately, quickly. This idiom comes from the military (also *at the double*), where it meant to march at double speed. From 1865: "Intellect not only marches, but marches at the 'double.' "

- Jerry told his kids to clean the house on the double.
- If your computer's broken, we'll fix it for you on the double.

154.

do a double take   *v. phr.*

To react late or to react a second time when you see or hear something strange or surprising.

- We had to do a double take when we saw Wendy's haircut.
- Hal did a double take when he saw his ten-year-old son in the driver's seat of the car.

155.

lead a double life   *v. phr.*

To have two lives, or to not tell the whole truth about one's life.

- Peter led a double life. He ran a trading company and had a normal family, but secretly he was a spy.
- The taxi driver led a double life. By day he was a driver, but by night he was an artist.

Quiz:

1. What is an occupation that makes people lead double lives?
2. What is something that might make a person do a double take?
3. Have you ever had to pull double duty, at work, at home, or in school?
4. Have you ever made a plan and then had second thoughts? What was the plan and what made you have second thoughts?

Idioms in the News

✎ "Visitors will do a **double-take** at portrait exhibit of famous Canadians." (Visitors will react at art exhibit.)
—Victoria Times Colonist (Canada), Mar. 25, 2013.

✎ "Argentine cleaner's **double life** as prize-winning writer." (Subway cleaner is also a prize-winning author.)
—Yahoo News / AFP, Mar. 24, 2016.

✎ "Bad dog? **Think twice** before yelling, experts say." (Advice on how to train pet dogs; avoid shouting.)
—Science Magazine, Nov. 6, 2019.

✎ "A grandmother's job is not to **second-guess** new parents." (Advice for grandparents: Don't give too much advice.)
—Washington Post, July 10, 2017.

✎ "Actors Do **Double Duty** in Oscar Films." (Some actors appear in two or three films that are nominated for Oscar Awards.)
—Wall Street Journal, Mar. 1, 2018.

✎ "North Carolina town may never fully recover from **double whammy** of storms." (Town of Fair Bluff hit by two hurricanes.)
—Reuters, Oct. 2, 2018.

✎ "8 Secrets for Taking a Romantic **Second Honeymoon** on the Cheap." (*On the cheap* means "inexpensively.")
—Reader's Digest (RD.com), July 26, 2019.

✎ "Up to one in three buyers of **second-hand** cars buys a lemon." (*Lemon* is slang for "a car that has many problems.")
—The Sydney Morning Herald, June 26, 2017.

✎ "For Speed, Chicago's Marathon Is **Second to None**." (The Chicago Marathan race is known as the world's fastest.)
—The New York Times, Oct. 11, 2019.

Review and Practice

Test Your Memory

Choose the best answer.

1. Mark almost won the race. He came in a ___.
   A. second guess
   B. close second
   C. second fiddle

2. Lisa wants to be the boss. She doesn't want to play ___ to anyone.
   A. second nature
   B. second class
   C. second fiddle

3. Pete has only enough money to buy a ___ car.
   A. second-class
   B. second-fiddle
   C. second-hand

4. I was tired, but I caught a ___.
   A. second wind
   B. second childhood
   C. second nature

5. Please complete the job right now, on the ___.
   A. second
   B. double
   C. twice

6. I was a business major, but I had ___ and switched to history.
   A. second guesses
   B. second thoughts
   C. twice thoughts

7. This restaurant's sushi is the best anywhere. It is ___.
   A. second best
   B. second to none
   C. not second

8. ___ before moving to the city.
   A. Think twice
   B. Second-guess
   C. Second thoughts

Good or Bad

For each idiom, choose G for a good situation or B for a bad one. When finished see the Answer Key.

1. second wind ___

2. second honeymoon ___

3. second childhood ___

4. think twice ___

5. double standard ___

6. see double ___

7. double over ___

8. double whammy ___

Quick Thought

As quickly as you can, think of an idiom that has the following meanings. When finished, check the Answer Key.

1. very much like something

2. used

3. unlikely to happen again

4. to return

5. to share a hotel room

6. bad in two ways

7. a vacation for an older couple

8. get cold feet

Section 6

The numbers three to seven give us numerous idioms. Some are good things: *three cheers, high five, a sixth sense* … But many are bad: *three strikes, third rail, and six feet under.* Good or bad, they add color to English.

Look at the idioms below. Underline phrases you don't know the meaning of? Then try to guess their meanings. Look at their words and try to figure them out. High five if you can.

- three-ring circus
- the three R's
- third rail
- third degree
- fourth estate
- between you, me … four walls
- four-letter word
- take five
- five o'clock shadow
- nickel-and-dime
- six feet under
- at sixes and sevens
- deep-six
- in seventh heaven

- three strikes
- three cheers
- third world
- third time's the charm
- the four corners of the earth
- on all fours
- high five
- take the Fifth
- five-and-dime
- fifth wheel
- six of one, half a dozen of …
- Joe Six-Pack
- sixth sense

Study the following pages until you get to the Review and Practice section on page 80. Then return to the list above to review idioms you underlined.

— Three and Up —

156.
three-ring circus   *n. phr.*

A scene that is confused, wild, and noisy. The term was used originally for circus performances that had three *rings,* or centers for performance, allowing for different acts at the same time (e.g., elephants, trapeze artists). For a confused scene, sometimes just *circus* is used.

- The conference was poorly planned. It was a three-ring circus!
- With four children, Kelly's life had turned into a bit of a circus.

The Circus: The word *circus* comes from Latin. It meant "circle." Modern circuses began in Europe in the 1700s. They typically are an arena (a place for performances or sports) in a tent. They have performances with elephants, lions, and other animals, and by people—acrobats with amazing physical skills and trapeze artists who swing through the air with ropes. In recent years, many famous circuses have been forced to close because of cruel treatment of animals.

157.
three strikes   *n. phr.*

More mistakes than are allowed. This idiom comes from baseball, where players have three chances to hit a well-thrown ball. If they fail, then they *strike out,* and it is another player's turn. Related idioms include *strike out,* meaning "to fail" and *have two strikes against (one),* which means "to be close to failing." These idioms show how popular the sport of baseball has been over the years.

- Our manager has made too many mistakes. It should be three strikes and you're out.
- Jack's professor has a three-strikes rule. If you miss three classes, you fail.

158.

the three R's *n. phr.*

Basic education: reading, writing, and arithmetic. It is said that in 1807, a London politician proposed a toast (a celebration drink) to the three R's, "reading, riting, and rithmetic," showing that he himself was not well educated. This idiom is also used outside of education and with other letters (see the second example).

- The small school didn't even teach the three R's.
- Remember the three P's of learning a language: practice, practice, and practice.

159.

three cheers (for) *phr.*

Good for. Used to express joy or approval. A *cheer* is a shout to show approval, such as at a football or baseball game. Three cheers is sometimes really three shouts in a row (see example one).

- Three cheers for the boss: hip, hip, hooray!
- Billy got the highest score on the exam, so let's all give three cheers to Billy.

160.

third rail *n. phr.*

An issue or a problem that people avoid because it's dangerous, often in politics. From railroads, when a third rail carries power.

- Public heath care is a third rail in many countries. People want it but it's very expensive.
- Which is better, Apple computers or PCs? That is a third rail for tech reporters.

161.

third world *n. phr.*

Developing countries. Often used as an adjective phrase. Sometimes capitalized: *Third World*. This idiom is common, but today is considered disparaging. A better term is *developing nations*.

- Viruses usually hit third-world countries the hardest.
- The charity works to improve education and health care in the Third World.

162.

third degree   *n. phr.*

Tough questioning such as the police might give someone they believe committed a crime. Often used with *give* and *get.*

- The police gave the suspect the third degree.
- When Billy came home after midnight, his mother gave him the third degree. (He got the third degree.)

163.

third time's the charm   *clause.*

The third try to do something will succeed (after one has failed twice). Also: *third time lucky.*

- Twice I've tried to persuade Peter to go with us, but I'll try again. Hopefully the third time's the charm.
- Carla ran for mayor twice and lost both elections. She's running again this year, hoping it will be third time lucky.

164.

fourth estate   *n. phr.*

The news media; the press. In Europe in history, society had three *estates*: the nobility, the clergy (church), and commoners (regular people). Sometimes the idea was also used for the *branches* of government—executive (president / prime minister), legislative (Parliament/Congress), and judicial (courts). When the news media became powerful in places like France, people then talked about a fourth power, the *fourth estate.*

- A smart president will always think about the fourth estate.
- When the legislature and the courts fail, people have to rely on the fourth estate.

165.

the four corners of the earth   *n. phr.*

Everywhere, in the farthest places. This idiom, which pictures the places farthest around the globe, appears in the Bible.

- Athletes from the four corners of the earth compete in the Olympics.
- Soon this software will be used in the four corners of the earth.

166.

between you, me, and the four walls *phr.*

In confidence; for you to know and no one else. This idiom is used to share secrets or give an opinion one doesn't want others to hear. Also: *between you and me, between you and me and the bedpost, between you and me and the gatepost.*

- Just between you and me (and the four walls), I heard Jenny and Bill are getting married.
- Just between you and me, our new manager is not very good.

167.

on all fours *adj. phr.*

On one's hands and knees on the ground. *Fours* refers to the four limbs (two legs and two arms). On all fours, one might be looking for something or crawling for some reason.

- Dan had to get down onto all fours on the ground to search for his contact lens.
- The boy was on all fours playing with the dog.

168.

four-letter word *n. phr.*

Short words that are *vulgar* (offensive language such as swearing and language about sex). This idiom is a polite way to refer to impolite language.

- Billy got into trouble at school for using a four-letter word in front of his teacher.
- Our general manager is often heard using four-letter words around the office.

169.

high five *n. phr., v. phr.*

A gesture where two people slap one hand each together in the air between them. Used for congratulations, such as in sports. Also a verb: *high-five*, and sometimes *low five*, with hands clapped low.

- When I scored a goal, the coach gave me a high five.
- This is an excellent lunch. You deserve a high five for preparing so much great food.

170.

take five *v. phr.*

Take a short break. Used in the imperative to tell people to stop working briefly and rest. Short for "take a five-minute break."

- OK, everyone, we've been working hard all morning. Let's take five and get some coffee.
- The movie director told us to take five.

Take Five: In 1959, the Dave Brubeck Quartet, a jazz group, recorded an album called *Time Out,* on which every song has an odd time signature (not 4/4, 3/4, or 2/4). The song *Take Five*, which is in 5/4 timing, was composed by Brubeck's saxophone player, Paul Desmond. A big hit, the song became a common jazz *standard* (a song played by many different musicians). Many versions can be heard free on YouTube.

171.

take the Fifth *v. phr.*

To refuse to answer questions because the answers would get one in trouble. This idiom comes from a law, the Fifth Amendment to the US Constitution, which says courts cannot force a person to answer questions that would get that person into trouble. The idiom is also used figuratively, outside courtrooms. Also: *plead the Fifth.*

- When the witness got into court, she said she was taking the Fifth, that she would not answer the lawyers' questions.
- "Did you eat the whole cake?" "I, uh, I'll have to take the Fifth on that question."

172.

five-o'clock shadow *n. phr.*

A man's face that is not clean shaven. This refers to whiskers many men have late in the day, many hours after shaving in the morning. With enough whiskers, the face appears to have a shadow.

- The stranger had a five-o'clock shadow.
- Ted had a five-o'clock shadow, so he ran home to shave.

173.

five-and-dime   *n. phr.*

A store that sells many inexpensive but often useful things. This term refers to *five* as in five cents and *dime*, a ten-cent coin (US). Today of course, you can't buy anything for ten cents or less, so the term is less common, though today the US has *dollar stores* and *ninety-nine-cent stores.*

- There used to be a five-and-dime next to the movie theater.
- The Dollar Tree is a popular chain of dollar stores.

> **Cheap Stores:** Many places have inexpensive stores like five-and-dimes, with similar names in different languages: 1,000 Little Things Store (Russia); One-Pound Shops (UK); Poundland (UK); 100-yen Shops (Japan); Annie's 60 Pence Bazaar (UK); Todo a 100 Stores (Spain); Serba Lima Ribu (All for 5,000, Indonesia); 100 Fils Stores (Kuwait).

174.

nickel-and-dime   *v. phr.*

To behave miserly (hating to spend money). To try to spend as little money as possible. This idiom refers to American five-cent (nickel) and ten-cent (dime) coins. Also an adjective, *nickel-and-dime*, meaning a cheap, low-quality operation. This latter is similar to *two-bit* (p. 53), which is slang for a quarter (twenty-five-cent coin).

- The company tried to nickel-and-dime it through the conference, and they looked very bad. It was a two-bit event.
- Peter runs a small nickel-and-dime company.

175.

fifth wheel   *n. phr.*

A person or thing that is unnecessary or extra. This idiom refers to an extra, unneeded wheel on a four-wheel vehicle.

- Since there were already two accountants, Nancy felt like a fifth wheel at the company.
- Frank wants to get a job where's he's needed. He doesn't want to be a fifth wheel.

176.
six feet under *adj. phr.*

Dead and buried. This idiom of course refers to the traditional depth at which bodies are buried (underground). Colloquial.

- No one can read my diary until I'm six feet under.
- Old Man Peters must be six feet under by now.

177.
six of one and half a dozen of the other *phr.*

It doesn't make a difference between two choices or things. Note that *dozen* means "twelve," so *six* and *half a dozen* are the same in number. Also: *two dozen* (24), *three dozen* (36), etc. Colloquial.

- You can take either highway and still get there in an hour. It's six of one and half a dozen of the other.
- I have no opinions on this. It's six of one to me.

178.
at sixes and sevens *adj. phr.*

Confused or disorganized. Some people believe this idiom came from a dice game where rolling a six or a seven had significance. This idiom was used by Chaucer in 1374. Colloquial.

- It seemed the world was at sixes and sevens that year.
- Pardon the mess. We just moved into this office two weeks ago, so we're still at sixes and sevens around here.

179.
Joe Six-Pack *n. phr.*

A common, ordinary person. A low- to middle-class man, wage earner, or blue-collar worker. A *six-pack* is six bottles or cans of beer sold together. The idiom pictures a blue-collar worker who goes home from work to a six-pack of beer in the evening. Similar terms include *Joe Schmo, Joe Blow, John Doe.*

- If you want to be mayor in this town, you have to win over Joe Six-Pack. It's a factory town.
- Opera doesn't appeal to Joe Six-Pack, so this part of the city is not a good location for an operahouse.

180.

deep-six *v. phr.*

To dispose of, to get rid of. This slang term comes from sailors who would call out the sea's depth as they measured it. *Deep six* refers to "six fathoms (6 X 1.8 meters) deep." The phrase also means "death" or "grave," especially burial at sea. Sometimes a noun: *the deep six*.

- If you don't wear a suit to the job interview, you'll deep-six your chances of getting the job.
- They knew that if the pirates caught them it would mean the deep six.

181.

sixth sense *n. phr.*

The ability to know what is going to or likely to happen, to predict events before other people. This phrase refers to a sense beyond the normal five senses (seeing, hearing, smelling, tasting, and feeling).

- Always invite Donna to sales meetings. When it comes to sales, she has a sixth sense.
- Mike got rich investing in stocks. When he's choosing companies to invest in, he seems to have a sixth sense.

182.

in seventh heaven *adj. phr.*

To be in a state of happiness and joy. This idiom comes from an ancient belief in the Middle East that there were seven heavens, a system recognized by both Muslims and ancient Jews. Also: *on cloud nine* (below).

- Helen was in seventh heaven when she learned her son was getting married. She wanted badly to be a grandmother.
- I'd be in seventh heaven if I could eat food this delicious every day. Your mother's a great cook.

Idioms in the News

✎ "On this day in sport: Real Madrid **in seventh heaven**." (Very happy football/soccer team).
—Yahoo Sports

Review and Practice

Test Your Memory

Choose the best answer.

1. Someone who gives you three cheers might also give you a ___.
   A. deep six
   B. high five
   C. fast four

2. We've been working for hours! Let's take ___ and get some coffee.
   A. three
   B. four
   C. five

3. The professor has a ___ rule; miss more than two classes and you fail.
   A. third-rail
   B. fourth-estate
   C. three-strikes

4. I was in ___ in my new sports car.
   A. sixes and sevens
   B. seventh heaven
   C. high five

5. Reading, writing, and arithmetic, the three ___.
   A. R's
   B. W's
   C. A's

6. Jimmy's mother gave him the ___ when he came home after midnight.
   A. fourth estate
   B. third degree
   C. fifth wheel

7. I'm not needed at our company anymore. I feel like a ___.
   A. fifth wheel
   B. fourth estate
   C. third rail

8. You won! Give me a ___.
   A. four-letter word
   B. high five
   C. third degree

Good or Bad

For each idiom, choose G for a good situation or B for a bad one. When finished see the explanation in the Answer Key.

1. three-ring circus ___

2. three strikes ___

3. three cheers ___

4. third rail ___

5. four-letter word ___

6. six feet under ___

7. take five ___

8. deep six ___

Quick Thought

As quickly as you can, think of an idiom that can have the following meanings. When finished, check the Answer Key.

1. confused, out of control

2. education

3. the press

4. crawling

5. save money

6. common people

7. able to tell the future

8. very happy

Section 7

Where does an *eight-hundred-pound gorilla* sit when it comes into a room? That is the *sixty-four-dollar question*. Also, if you *dress to the nines*, why will you look like more than nine dollars?

Sometimes, the larger the number in an idiom, the more color it adds to speaking and writing.

Look at the idioms below. Underline phrases you don't know the meaning of. Then try to guess their meanings. Look at their words and try to figure them out.

- on cloud nine
- whole nine yards
- possession is nine-tenths of …
- not touch with a ten-foot pole
- ten-four
- a dime a dozen
- catch-22
- forty winks
- sixty-four-dollar question
- eight-hundred-pound gorilla
- like a million dollars
- million miles away from
- a million to one

- dressed (up) to the nines
- a stitch in time saves nine
- count to ten
- ten to one
- eleventh hour
- fifteen minutes of fame
- twenty-four seven (24/7)
- go fifty-fifty
- ninety-nine times out of …
- bat a thousand
- not in a million years
- a million and one
- chance in a million

Study the following pages until you get to the Review and Practice section on page 91. Then return to the list above to review idioms you underlined.

183.

on cloud nine *adj. phr.*

Very happy. It's unclear why *nine* is used; sometimes it's *cloud seven*, possibly from *seventh heaven*. Numerous songs, albums, movies, TV shows, and even a *League of Legends* e-sports team have Cloud Nine in their name. Also: *seventh heaven* (above).

- Kim has been on cloud nine ever since she moved to the big city.
- His first time at the new restaurant, Dick was on cloud nine as he tasted each new dish … on cloud nine, that is, until he saw the bill.

184.

dressed (up) to the nines *v. phr.*

To be wearing formal, fancy clothes. *To the nines* was used by the 1700s to mean "to the most or the highest degree." By the 1800s it was used with *dress*. Today, you still see *dressed to the nines,* though the variation *dressed to kill* is more common. Note that the phrasal verb *dress up* by itself is commonly used to mean "wear formal clothes," as in "Always dress up for job interviews."

- Everyone at the opera was dressed to the nines.
- The band's singer was dressed to kill.

185.

whole nine yards *n. phr.*

Everything. All the way. This idiom may have come from a humorous 1855 story called "The Judge's Big Shirt," in which a judge orders a shirt and when it arrives, it is far too large. Then the judge says: "What a silly, stupid woman! I told her to get just enough to make three shirts; instead of making three, she has put the whole nine yards into one shirt!"

- Sherry did a great job of planning the conference. She went the whole nine yards, ordering food, drinks, entertainment, and even gifts for everyone who attended.
- Vic's father took all sorts of stuff with them on the camping trip: tents, sleeping bags, a camping stove, fishing poles … the whole nine yards!

186.
a stitch in time (saves nine) *phr.*

It is better to act early to prevent trouble, or to solve problems immediately, before they get worse. This idiom appeared in a 1732 collection of proverbs. Often shortened to just *a stitch in time*.

- Computer hackers can cost companies a lot of money, so let's get some good security software. A stitch in time, after all.
- I change the oil on my car every six months. You know the saying: "A stitch in time saves nine."

187.
possession is nine-tenths of the law *clause.*

Having something is the most important factor in deciding who keeps it, when two or more people want it. Also: *Possession is nine points of the law*. The *points* are things a person needs to win a lawsuit, such as evidence, good witnesses, a good judge, etc.

- Ben and Tim both say they own a set of tools from their old business. Ben asked Tim to give them to him, but Tim said, "Possession is nine-tenths of the law."
- With trade secrets, possession is nine-tenths of the law.

188.
count to ten *v. phr.*

Calm down, get control of your emotions. Used in the imperative when someone is upset or angry. The idea is that resting for the time it takes to count to ten will calm someone down.

- OK, you're angry at the news, but count to ten before you speak, so you don't say something you'll be sorry about.
- When I heard the news, I told myself, "Count to ten."

189.
not touch (something) with a ten-foot pool *v. phr.*

To stay away from, to avoid. This idiom goes back to the mid-1700s. It pictures fear or distrust and not wanting to get near something.

- I'm careful about what stocks I invest in, and that company is poorly run. I wouldn't touch its stock with a ten-foot pole.
- As a kid, Ned wouldn't touch vegetables with a ten-foot pole.

190.

ten to one   *adv. phr.*

Most likely, certainly. This idiom expresses odds, ten to one, as if making a bet, but it is used figuratively as a sentence adverb meaning simply "I think." Also: *ten-to-one odds*. These phrases go back to at least the late 1500s. Similar: *I bet ...*

- Ten to one Fred will be late again today. He hates Monday mornings.
- Look at those clouds. Ten to one it'll be raining by the time we arrive at the park. I bet it'll be raining.

191.

ten-four   *phr.*

I understand; message received. Used to show understanding. This phrase comes from citizens band (CB) radio, where it has just that meaning. Today it's also used figuratively, beyond radio.

- "Let's meet at nine o'clock tomorrow morning, OK?" "Ten-four."
- "Did you receive the message?" "Ten-four."

192.

eleventh hour   *n. phr.*

At the last possible time or minute. This idiom goes back to Old English and likely comes from the Bible, referring to the eleventh hour of a twelve-hour work day. Also an adjective: *eleventh-hour*.

- The two companies made an agreement at the eleventh hour.
- Everyone was surprised by the eleventh-hour decision to cancel the event.

193.

a dime a dozen   *phr.*

Of little value because there are so many. *Dozen* means "twelve" or "group of twelve," a term dating from at least the 1300s. It is also used in the plural to mean a large number of something: "Dozens of people agreed." The *dime* was made the American 10-cent coin in 1786. If you can buy a dozen of something for 10 cents, it has little value.

- These days, people with basic computer skills are a dime a dozen. You need more than that to get a great job.
- Suggestions are a dime a dozen; what we need is action.

194.
fifteen minutes of fame *n. phr.*

A brief period of time when one is famous or getting attention. Sometimes just *fifteen minutes*.

- Jack had his fifteen minutes of fame as a college athlete, but he never played professional sports.
- Well, you won the poetry contest. Enjoy your fifteen minutes.

195.
catch-22 *n. phr.*

A difficult situation that cannot be solved. *Catch* here means a difficulty or complication (Catch No. 22). This idiom comes from the 1961 satirical war novel by Joseph Heller, named *Catch-22*. In it, an American pilot during World War II wants to escape the war and tells an army doctor he is insane because of the danger. But he is told his desire to avoid danger shows that he is in fact quite sane.

- You can't get a job without experience and you can't get experience without a job—it's a real catch-22.
- Sarah found herself in a catch-22 situation.

195.
twenty-four seven (24/7) *adv. phr., adj. phr.*

Nonstop, twenty-four hours a day, seven days a week. This idiom is usually written in numerals: *24/7*. Originally used for stores that stay open all night, but later for anything.

- The police department is keeping our city safe 24/7.
- Our supermarket is open 24/7. We never close.

196.
forty winks *n. phr.*

A brief nap. This idiom dates from the early 1800s. *Wink* is an older term that meant "sleep"; it is still used in phrases like I *didn't sleep a wink* (not even a little bit).

- I need to grab forty winks. I didn't get a wink of sleep last night, so I'm exhausted.
- Forty winks and Pauline felt as good as new.

197.

go fifty-fifty *v. phr.*

To share costs. *Fifty* here refers to 50 percent. See also: *go halves* (above). For restaurants or dates, *go Dutch* is often used. Compare: *fifty-fifty chance*, as in "We have a fifty-fifty chance of winning."

- If we go fifty-fifty, we can afford to rent a car in Paris.
- We went fifty-fifty when we bought the car, so we have fifty-fifty ownership.

> **Fifty-fifty:** Just as two people can *go fifty-fifty*, they can also *go sixty-forty*, *seventy-thirty*, etc. These expressions are often used to talk about profits: "We split the profits from our company *fifty-fifty* (or *sixty-forty*, etc.)." Probability is said in the same way: *a fifty-fifty chance* of winning, etc.

198.

sixty-four-dollar question *n. phr.*

The important question at the moment, a difficult question. Also: *$64 question*. This idiom comes from a US radio quiz show on which the final question offered a sixty-four-dollar prize. The show, "Take It or Leave It," ran from 1940–1948. At the time, $64 was a lot of money. Later quiz shows and TV game shows had to offer larger prizes, and this idiom has changed too. A 1950 radio quiz show was called "$64,000 Question," also the name of a 1955 TV show. The idiom is now sometimes *sixty-four-thousand-dollar question* and *million-dollar question*.

- With Nancy retiring, how can our company find as good of a manager—that's the sixty-four-dollar question.
- This is definitely our dream home. The million-dollar question is how can we afford it?

> **Pyramid:** An American TV game show called "$10,000 Pyramid" aired in 1973. The largest prize was $10,000. The name was later changed to "$20,000 Pyramid," then "$50,000 Pyramid," then in 2016, "$100,000 Pyramid."

199.
ninety-nine times out of a hundred *adv. phr.*

Almost always; the majority of the time. Also: *ninety-nine cases, people*, etc. Compare: "Nine out of ten people prefer coffee over tea." "Eight out of ten students knew the answer."

- Jimmy says he's too sick to go to school today? Ninety-nine times out of a hundred he just doesn't want to go.
- Ninety-nine people out of a hundred know the world is round.

200.
eight-hundred-pound gorilla *n. phr.*

A person or organization that is dominating or cannot be controlled because of its size or power. Spelled with numerals or words (*800* or *eight hundred*). Sometimes: *800-pound gorilla in the room*. This idiom comes from an old joke that asks, "Where does an 800-pound gorilla sit?" Answer: "Wherever it wants."

- The telephone company is the eight-hundred-pound gorilla that we have to reform.
- Our country uses a lot more energy than others, so when it comes to fighting global warming, we're the 800-pound gorilla in the room.

201.
bat a thousand *v. phr.*

To have a perfect record; to be very successful over time. This idiom comes from the sport of baseball. *To bat* means to try to hit balls with a bat. Each player has a *batting average,* which is the number of balls the player hits, divided by the number of *at bats* (turns batting). A batting average of .300 is considered good; .400 is nearly impossible. Batting a thousand would be perfect. People began using this idiom figuratively outside of baseball by the 1920s.

- Our new sales rep is batting a thousand. She's made a sale with each customer she's met with.
- As a student, Lisa insisted on batting a thousand on attendance. She never missed a single class.

> **Million:** *Million* has been used to mean "an uncertain but very large number/amount" for the past two centuries. More and more, *billion* and *trillion* are being used for this, so we might say "She looks like a *trillion* dollars" (instead of *million*). Sometimes people also use *zillion* to mean "a huge number": "I can think of a zillion reasons to learn English."

202.

like a million dollars *adv. phr.*

Very beautiful or good. This North American idiom expresses how someone looks or feels. Also: *like a million bucks* (*buck* is a common US term for "dollar"). In the early 1900s several popular novelists used this expression: "... I had just climbed out from under the cold shower feeling like a million dollars" (P. G. Wodehouse, 1925).

- Fred felt like a million dollars after a long nap.
- Verna looks like million dollars in her new dress.

203.

not in a million years *adv. phr.*

Never; under no circumstances. Also: *never in a million years*. This expression dates from the early 1900s.

- A lot of people got sick at that restaurant on its opening night. I wouldn't eat there in a million years.
- Kevin would never in a million years do anything to upset his family.

204.

million miles away from *phr.*

Very far, very different. This phrase pictures a long distance, but it is used figuratively to mean "very different." *A million miles* also means "a high degree,"or "very much" (see example two).

- Her latest book is a million miles away from her last one.
- That's the number one question by a million miles.

205.

a million and one *adj. phr.*

A great many, a very large number of people or things. Here, *million* is used as an amount that is overwhelming.

- Kate knew a million and one people at the party; I didn't know anyone.
- I have a million and one things to do today.

206.

a million to one *adv. phr.*

Very unlikely; a low probability. This phrase pictures the odds or chances of something happening (one chance in a million). Often used as an adjective: *million-to-one chance.*

- The project doesn't have even a million-to-one chance of being completed on time.
- The chances of seeing someone I knew while I was in Paris were a million to one against.

207.

chance in a million *n. phr.*

Very unlikely, a low probability. Also: *one in a million.*

- There wasn't a chance in a million that any of the students could have explained the answer.
- It was a chance in a million that no one was hurt in the fire.

Large Numbers: Numbers larger than 100,000 (US):

- million (1,000,000)
- billion (1,000,000,000)
- trillion (1,000,000,000,000)
- quadrillion (1,000,000,000,000,000)
- quintillion (1,000,000,000,000,000,000)
- sextillion (1,000,000,000,000,000,000,000)
- septillion (1,000,000,000,000,000,000,000,000)
- octillion (1,000,000,000,000,000,000,000,000,000)

Idioms in the News

- "**Three cheers** for the onion." (A look at the popularity of onions in history.)
  —BBC News, Jan. 4, 2015.

- "Dental Care in England '**Third World**.'" (Some people say the UK has poor dental care. This headline calls it "third world," or not modern.)
  —BBC News, Jan. 4, 2016.

- "Kale is a **four-letter word**—but why?" (Article on how the vegetable kale is unpopular, and is like a bad word to many.)
  —The Guardian, July 8, 2014.

- "Government Officials Should Not Be Allowed to **Plead the Fifth**." (Opinion on officials refusing to answer questions.)
  —Forbes, June 2, 2013.

- "For Diners, It's **Seventh Heaven**." (Article about the many restaurants in downtown Los Angeles. *Diner* = people eating.)
  —LA DT News, Oct. 8, 2010.

- "Hong Kong's aging master tailors need a **stitch in time**." (Hong Kong is famous for tailors, but few young people want to enter the trade, so the reputation may soon be lost.)
  —Reuters, Feb. 26, 2015.

- "Ideas Are a **Dime a Dozen**. People Who Implement Them are Priceless." (We have many ideas, but not enough people carrying ideas out.)
  —Forbes, Mar. 14, 2013.

- "Google is still the **800-pound gorilla**." (Article on Google, IBM, and Microsoft as dominant tech companies.)
  —Consumer Watchdog, 2010.

Review and Practice

Test Your Memory

Choose the best answer.

1. Always update your security software. Remember: ___ ...
   A. a stitch in time
   B. the whole nine years
   C. a dime a dozen

2. Look at those clouds! ___ it's going to rain this afternoon.
   A. Forty winks
   B. Ten to one
   C. Count to ten

3. People with computer skills are easy to find today. They're ___.
   A. batting a thousand
   B. a dime a dozen
   C. a nickel and dime

4. I was on ___ in my new apartment.
   A. a whole nine yards
   B. cloud nine
   C. forty winks

5. Wendy has a perfect attendance record. She's ___.
   A. batting a thousand
   B. counting to ten
   C. like a million dollars

6. Jake's restaurant is very special. It's ___.
   A. a million to one
   B. a million and one
   C. one in a million

7. Not in a million ___ would I jump out of an airplane!
   A. miles
   B. years
   C. dollars

8. If you're sleepy, you should grab ___.
   A. ten-four
   B. forty winks
   C. eleventh hour

Good or Bad

For each idiom, choose G for a good situation for B or a bad one. When finished see the Answer Key.

1. cloud nine ___

2. stitch in time ___

3. a dime a dozen ___

4. batting a thousand ___

5. forty winks ___

6. eight-hundred-pound gorilla ___

7. one in a million ___

8. twenty-four seven ___

Quick Thought

As quickly as you can, think of an idiom that can have the following meanings. When finished, check the Answer Key.

1. very common

2. everything

3. I understand

4. my guess is

5. unique

6. unwilling

7. beautiful

8. always, constantly

Answer Key

Section 1, p. 21. Crossword Puzzle

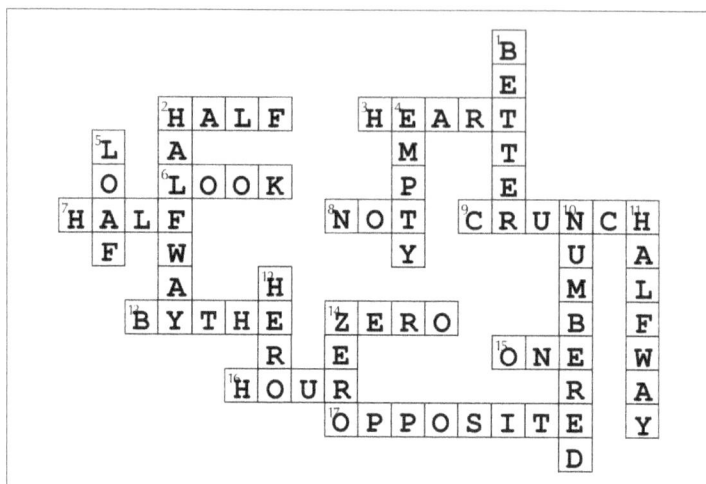

```
                                              ¹B
                                               E
          ²H A L F        ³H ⁴E A R T          T
    ⁵L    A              M    T
     O    ⁶L O O K       P    E
  ⁷H A L F              ⁸N O T   ⁹C R U N C ¹⁰H ¹¹
     F    W              Y          U    A
          A    ¹²H                  M    L
        ¹³B Y T H E    ¹⁴Z E R O     B    F
          R    E         E      ¹⁵O N E    W
        ¹⁶H O U R        Z           R    A
              ¹⁷O P P O S I T E      Y
                                     D
```

Section 1, p. 22. Test Your Memory

Choose the best answer.

1. Jill said, "He can't fool me! I've got his number." She means she _C_.

2. My father told me to look out for No. 1. This means I should _B_.

3. The mayor will meet with her opposite number in New York. She's going to meet with _C_.

4. We have to decide now. It's _C_.

5. Dan worked here for a year before I met his better half, before I _C_.

6. The kids did a number on the kitchen. They _B_.

7. "Who ate my cake?" "Any number of people could have eaten it." This means _B_.

8. Let's split the dinner bill; let's _B_.

Section 1, p. 22. Good or Bad

1. (one's) days are numbered: Bad.

2. do a number on: Bad. It's a bad thing to do.

3. safety in numbers: Good. Safety is good.

4. with half a heart: Bad. But sometimes unavoidable.

5. go halfway: Good.

6. not half bad: Good.

7. from zero to hero: Good.

8. glass is half empty: Bad. Usually bad.

Section 1, p. 22. Quick Thought

1. split a restaurant bill: go Dutch, go halves.

2. (do) reluctantly: with half a heart.

3. suddenly become famous: from zero to hero.

4. tasty: not half bad.

5. focus on: zero in on.

6. harm: do a number on.

7. follow the rules: by the numbers, by the book.

8. time to do something: zero hour.

Section 2, p. 32. Test Your Memory

1. The storm was bad, but everyone got to work safely, _B_.

2. The used-car salesman tried to pull a fast one on us. He tried to _A_.

3. If my company is a one-man show, how many hats do I wear? _B_.

4. The café is one of a kind. It _C_.

5. Our boss loved Kyle's sales plan. Kyle _B_.

6. Everything's been going wrong today. It's been _B_.

7. My cat always wants to eat. She has a _A_.

8. My plan failed, so it's _A_.

Section 2, p. 32. Good or Bad

1. A-one: Good. Perfect.

2. one too many: Bad.

3. all in one piece: Good.

4. pull a fast one: Bad. A bad thing to do.

5. one of those days: Bad.

6. at one (with): Good.

7. hole in one: Good. Great.

8. in one ear and out the other: Bad.

Section 2, p. 32. Quick Thought

1. comfortable: at one with.

2. start over: back to square one.

3. remarkable: one of a kind, one for the books.

4. all at once: at one fell swoop.

5. safely: in one piece.

6. a big accomplishment: hole in one.

7. doesn't listen: in one ear and out the other.

8. top quality: A-1.

Section 3, p. 44. Test Your Memory

1. _A_, I didn't understand, but once the teacher explained, I got it.

2. Teaching is more important to me than publishing; I am _B_ a teacher.

3. The teacher met with each student individually; they met _B_.

4. Enter one at a time, or _C_.

5. Images are very important in books. One picture is _C_.

6. Our company is always _B_ of other companies; we always beat them.

7. We will succeed somehow. We'll find a way. We'll succeed _C_.

8. We had a bad start. We didn't _B_.

Section 3, p. 44. Good or Bad

1. love at first sight: Maybe good. Maybe bad.

2. one arm tied behind (one's) back: Good. Talented.

3. one jump ahead: Good.

4. one foot in the grave: Bad. Very bad.

5. (teach) one on one: Good.

6. one in a million: Good.

7. one of the boys: Good.

8. not get to first base: Bad.

Section 3, p. 44. Quick Thought

1. (do) with agreement: with one voice.

2. everyone: one and all.

3. individually: one by one.

4. personally: at first hand.

5. unique: one in a million.

6. not worth seeing: If you've seen one, you've seen them all.

7. accepted, friendly with others: one of the boys.

8. very ill: one foot in the grave.

Section 4, p. 55. Crossword Puzzle.

Section 4, p. 56. Test Your Memory

1. You keep changing your mind. Please decide _B_ what you want to do.

2. The job offer was a once-in-a-lifetime opportunity. It was _C_.

3. If Donny is two-faced, you know you _A_.

4. I think we should go. That's my _B_.

5. I gave the coat the _B_ before I bought it, to see if it was damaged.

6. Kim thinks it is too hot to work? So do I, so that _A_.

7. Tim didn't have a lot of money, so he had to stay in a _C_ hotel.

8. I am certain. There's no _A_ it.

Section 4, p. 56. Good or Bad

1. stand on (one's) own two feet: Good.

2. two's company: Good.

3. two strikes against (one): Bad.

4. fool (someone): Bad. Bad thing to do.

5. two-faced: Bad.

6. two wrongs: Bad. They don't make a right.

7. two left feet: Bad. Unless you just don't like dancing.

8. of two minds: Bad.

Section 4, p. 56. Quick Thought

1. person who follows rules: Goody Two-Shoes.

2. figure out: put two and two together.

3. extremely rare: once in a blue moon, once in a lifetime.

4. I agree: That makes two of us.

5. my opinion: my two cents.

6. twenty-five cents: two bits.

7. already in trouble: have two strikes against (one).

8. can't dance: have two left feet.

Section 5, p. 70. Test Your Memory

1. Mark almost won the race. He came in a _B_.

2. Lisa wants to be the boss. She doesn't want to play _C_ to anyone.

3. Pete has only enough money to buy a _C_ car.

4. I was tired, but I caught a _A_.

5. Please complete the job right now, on the _B_.

6. I was a business major, but I had _B_ and switched to history.

7. This restaurant's sushi is the best anywhere. It is _B_.

8. _A_ before moving to the city.

Section 5, p. 70. Good or Bad

1. second wind: Good.

2. second honeymoon: Good.

3. second childhood: Maybe good, maybe bad.

4. think twice: Good. Usually good.

5. double standard: Bad.

6. see double: Bad.

7. double over: Bad. Unless you're laughing. Then good.

8. double whammy: Bad.

Section 5, p. 70. Quick Thought

1. very much like something: second cousin.

2. used: second hand.

3. unlikely to happen again: Lightning never strikes in the same place twice.

4. to return: double back.

5. to share a hotel room: double up.

6. bad in two ways: double whammy.

7. a vacation for an older couple: second honeymoon.

8. get cold feet: have second thoughts.

Section 6, p. 80. Test Your Memory

1. Someone who gives you three cheers might also give you a _B_.

2. We've been working for hours! Let's take _C_ and get some coffee.

3. The professor has a _C_ rule; miss more than two classes and you fail.

4. I was in _B_ in my new sports car.

5. Reading, writing, and arithmetic, the three _A_.

6. Jimmy's mother gave him the _B_ when he came home after midnight.

7. I'm not needed at our company anymore. I feel like a _A_.

8. You won! Give me a _B_.

Section 6, p. 80. Good or Bad

1. three-ring circus: Bad.

2. three strikes: Bad.

3. three cheers: Good.

4. third rail: Bad.

5. four-letter word: Bad. But not uncommon.

6. six feet under: Very Bad.

7. take five: Good.

8. deep six: Bad.

Section 6, p. 80. Quick Thought
1. confused, out of control: three-ring circus.
2. education: the three R's.
3. the press: the fourth estate.
4. crawling: on all fours.
5. save money: nickel-and-dime.
6. common people: Joe Six-Pack.
7. able to tell the future: sixth sense.
8. very happy: on cloud nine, in seventh heaven.

Section 7, p. 91. Test Your Memory
1. Always update your computer's security software. Remember: _A_ ...
2. Look at those clouds! _B_ it's going to rain this afternoon.
3. People with computer skills are easy to find today. They're _B_.
4. I was on _B_ in my new apartment.
5. Wendy has a perfect attendance record. She's _A_.
6. Jake's restaurant is very special. It's _C_.
7. Not in a million _B_ would I jump out of an airplane!
8. If you're sleepy, you should grab _B_.

Section 7, p. 91. Good or Bad
1. cloud nine: Good.
2. stitch in time: Good.
3. a dime a dozen: Maybe good, maybe bad.
4. batting a thousand: Good.
5. forty winks: Usually good.
6. eight-hundred-pound gorilla: Usually bad.
7. one in a million: Good.
8. twenty-four seven: Usually good.

Section 7, p. 91. Quick Thought
1. very common: dime a dozen.
2. everything: the whole nine yards.
3. I understand: ten-four.
4. my guess is: ten to one.
5. unique: one in a million.
6. unwilling: not for a million dollars.
7. beautiful: look like a million dollars.
8. always, constantly: twenty-four seven.

Alphabetical List of Idioms

Dictionary Vocabulary

Intermediate- and advanced-level students of English should learn the basic vocabulary that dictionaries use to explain words. Knowing this vocabulary will make reference books and online matrials easier to use. Below are terms used often in this book.

Languages.
- Ancient Greek. The language spoken in ancient Greece.
- Latin. The language spoken in ancient Rome.
- Old English. English from the fifth to the eleventh century.
- Middle English. English from around 1150 to 1500.
- Modern English. English from 1500 forward.

Dictionary Talk. This book uses common dictionary vocabulary, terms that students should become familiar with. Below are a few.

- Chaucer. Middle English writer.
- colloquial, *adj.* Informal spoken English.
- date from, *phrasal verb*. Was in use by (time). Also: *goes back to.*
- figurative, *adj.* (Used) for topics other than the normal meaning.
- figuratively, *adv.* Not in the literal, or normal, meaning.
- imperative, *n.* Imperative mood, used for instructions (e.g., "Sit.")
- slang, *adj.* Informal, nonstandard English.
- in the negative, *adv. phr.* Actions not done, as with *not, never*, etc.
- in the plural, *adv. phr.* With a plural noun.
- modify, *v.* To change the meaning of other words (e.g., Adj. + N.).
- negative, *adj.* Has a bad meaning, calls something bad.
- passive voice, *n.* A clause with a subject that's acted on by the verb.
- positive, *adj.* Has a good meaning, calls something good.
- proverb, *n.* An old saying, often a full clause, usually giving advice.
- Shakespeare. Early Modern English writer, inventor of many idioms.

Free Online English Dictionaries

Intermediate English learners should begin using English-English as well as bilingual dictionaries (e.g., English-Spanish or English-Chinese). There are excellent online dictionaries from the top reference book publishers, some of them designed for English learners and some with multiple languages. Most are free.

In addition to definitions, online dictionaries offer English lessons, word games, blogs, word-of-the-day emails, quizzes, and other features. Below is an introduction to some of the best. Try using dictionary websites like these alongside books like this one.

Learner's and multilingual dictionaries

Collins Cobuild

Collins has long published excellent dictionaries for English learners. Covering both British and American English (with explanations), Collins's print dictionaries offer easy-to-understand definitions, detailed parts-of-speech labels, and example sentences taken from real sources, showing words and terms in actual use.

Collins's online dictionary offers definitions in English as well as European languages, Hindi, and Chinese. This allows learners to get both English-English and bilingual definitions. The website also offers synonyms, a translator, an English grammar section, and games.

Many search results have tabs to click for American English, British English, (real) examples, video pronunciation, word lists, and instant definitions in most major languages. All free online.

⇨ Website: www.collinsdictionary.com

Merriam-Webster Learner's Dictionary

Merriam-Webster is a leading publisher of American English reference books. Its dictionaries are the spelling authority for most American book and magazine publishers, and its main online dictionary is where many people go for spelling and other details.

Going online, Merriam-Webster expanded into related publications with its Learner's ESL Dictionary; Spanish Central, a Spanish dictionary; Word Central for Kids; and its Visual Dictionary.

Only Merriam-Webster's dictionaries are directly related to the original Webster's books, first published by Noah Webster (1758–1843). Still, other publishers use the Webster name.

The company's online Learner's Dictionary has numerous features for people studying the language. All free.

⇨ Website (Regular): merriam-webster.com

⇨ Website (Learner's): learnersdictionary.com

Cambridge Learner's Dictionary

Cambridge University Press has built an impressive website with English-English definitions as well as definitions in multiple European and Asian languages. It also has a translation tool, a grammar reference, and other features.

⇨ Website: dictionary.cambridge.org

Oxford Learner's Dictionaries

Oxford University Press has a learner's dictionary website with a variety of features including a text checker and a grammar reference.

⇨ Website: www.oxfordlearnersdictionaries.com

Standard American English dictionaries

Webster's New World Dictionary

This is the official dictionary and spelling authority of the Associated Press and most news organizations in the US and online. That makes it, along with Merriam-Webster's, the most important reference for American English. Note that several publishers use the name Webster (from Noah Webster) in dictionary names. Webster's New World is published by Wiley Publishing. It is available free online at YourDictionary.com.

⇨ Website: www.yourdictionary.com

American Heritage Dictionary

This dictionary was published as an alternative to Merriam-Webster's and is the favorite word reference of many teachers and writers. It is known for excellent definitions and word usage advice from its Usage Panel, a large group of writers, public speakers, and people who work with words. The American Heritage Dictionary is known also for beautiful print editions and is available for free online.

⇨ Website: www.ahdictionary.com

Macmillan Dictionary

Macmillan's website offers its regular dictionary alongside an "open dictionary," which people can add words to, and a variety of English language resources.

⇨ Website: www.macmillandictionary.com

OneLook

OneLook searches for definitons in more than a thousand online dictionaries including Merriam-Webster's, Webster's New World, Oxford Dictionaries, American Heritage, Cambridge, Macmillan, and numerous specialized dictionaries.

⇨ Website: www.onelook.com

www.ingramcontent.com/pod-product-compliance
Lightning Source LLC
Chambersburg PA
CBHW051734040426

42447CB00008B/1132